THEY SHAPED OUR WORSHIP

THEY SHAPED OUR WORSHIP

Essays on Anglican Liturgists

Edited by
CHRISTOPHER IRVINE

Alcuin Club Collections 75

First published in Great Britain 1998
Society for Promoting Christian Knowledge
Holy Trinity Church
Marylebone Road
London NW1 4DU

Alcuin Club Collections 75

British Library Cataloguing-in-Publication Data

A catalogue record for this book is available from
the British Library

ISBN 0-281-05095-3

Typeset by Pioneer Associates, Perthshire
Printed in Great Britain at
The University Printing House, Cambridge

CONTENTS

CONTRIBUTORS

Paul Bradshaw is Professor of Liturgy in the University of Notre Dame, and is currently Director of Studies of the Notre Dame House of Studies in London. His recent publications include *The Search for the Origins of Christian Worship*.

Colin Buchanan is Bishop of Woolwich, chair of the Alcuin/GROW editorial board, and editor of *News of Liturgy*.

Richard Buxton was until recently Sub-Warden of Saint Deiniol's Library, Hawarden.

Anne Dawtry is Senior Chaplain at Bournemouth University, and a member of the *PRAXIS* Council.

Martin Dudley is Rector of the Priory Church of St Bartholomew the Great, London, and has written extensively on liturgy and sacramental theology.

Donald Gray is a Canon of Westminster, and Rector of St Margaret's, Westminster. He has recently published a biography of Ronald Jasper.

Christopher Irvine is Vicar of Cowley St John, Oxford, and chairman of the Diocesan Liturgical Committee. He recently edited *Celebrating the Easter Mystery*.

Gordon Jeanes is Sub-Warden of St Michael's College, Llandaff, and lectures in Liturgy and Church History in University College, Cardiff.

Ruth Meyers is Assistant Professor of Liturgics at Seabury-Western Theological Seminary, Illinois, USA.

Michael Moriarty is an Adjunct Assistant Professor of Liturgy in the University of Notre Dame, USA.

Bridget Nichols is a research student in the University of Durham.

Phillip Tovey is a Diocesan Liturgy Adviser and Priest in Charge of a group of rural parishes on the outskirts of Oxford. He is a member of GROW.

Gordon Wakefield was formerly Principal of Queen's College, Birmingham.

INTRODUCTION

This collection of essays has been published to mark the centenary of the Alcuin Club, a club founded in 1897 by four laymen, Dr J. Wickham Legg, H. B. Briggs, W. H. St John Hope, and J. T. Micklethwaite. Its aim was to promote the study of the English liturgical tradition, with a specific focus on the Book of Common Prayer. This it has sought to do through publishing and the dissemination of liturgical scholarship, and during its hundred-year history it has been involved in the publication of some two hundred publications. At the time of the inception of the Club, the Church of England had emerged from a twenty-year period of ritual controversy in which the 'Lincoln Judgement' of 1890 was a watershed. The bishop of Lincoln, Edward King, had been charged with the illegal use of various ceremonial practices, but Archbishop Benson allowed the re-examination of the practices, which allegedly contravened the directives of the Prayer Book, and only the signing of the cross was deemed to be illegal. The whole unhappy episode raised the need for a greater liturgical awareness amongst the clergy and people of the Church of England, and this the Club sought to address.

This present volume presents a series of essays on those who have now died, but who have contributed to liturgical scholarship and the renewal of liturgical practice and the conduct of worship during the lifetime of the Club. Many of the subjects in this collection will be known and remembered; others have been forgotten or ignored, and in an age when there is a propensity to reinvent the wheel, it is good that the contribution of these figures should be set down and critically evaluated.

The gallery presented here falls into four groups. First, there were those like Brightman and Walter Frere, who were engaged in scholarly research. The second group includes those like John Wickham Legg, Percy Dearmer and Vernon Staley, who, though limited by their antiquarian fascination and narrow vision of English religious practice, were concerned with the setting and conduct of worship. The third group includes Gabriel Hebert, and Palmer Ladd in the United States, who, through their ecumenical contacts, work and writings, brought to the Anglican Church the insights of the Continental Liturgical Movement, and helped to create the climate in which the process of liturgical revision could productively proceed. Finally, of course, there were those such as Edward Ratcliff and Ronald Jasper, who were in the vanguard of liturgical revision and members of the Church of England Liturgical Commission.

Needless to say, a grouping of subjects in this way is a fairly artificial categorization, because as the reader will discover, a number of the figures who feature in this volume will appear, as it were, in more than one room of the gallery. So, rather than grouping the essays under various headings (one might, for instance, have used 'academic', 'ecclesiastic', 'liturgical wordsmith', and 'creator of sacred space' as possible headings), they have been arranged in chronological order. Each essay offers a biographical sketch, an evaluation of the subject's contribution to scholarship or the renewal of worship, and attempts to show the bearing that contribution has upon current liturgical concerns and practice.

However, in the bringing together of these four groups, a more general picture of the different aims and desirable settings of liturgical study and writing begins to emerge. The first point represents the serious academic engagement with the various historic traditions of the Church's worship, a task which presupposes considerable linguistic competence, and a broad grasp of theology, as well as the skills of the historical critic. Such solid academic endeavour, undertaken in an age of increasing subject specialism, demands that the academic liturgical scholar is in close dialogue with those of other disciplines, such as historians, linguists and anthropologists. This, of course, requires a real partnership and meeting of minds, and should not be reduced to the exercise of liturgists simply adopting the methodologies of other disciplines for their own needs and purposes. Liturgical scholarship, in other words, cannot simply be a question of liturgists talking to other liturgists.

Second, those who write liturgy and have the responsibility of planning and leading worship need to be informed of current liturgical research, but despite the protestations of some, liturgy is in another sense too important to be left in the academy. Liturgy is not the text discussed in the seminar, or analysed on the liturgist's desk. It is the corporate prayer of the people of God and the sacramental expression of God's redemptive care through pastoral ministrations to those in the wider community. In other words, liturgy is something that is *done*, and therefore equal attention needs to be given to how it is done, and the physical setting of the rites of the Church, which mediate God's saving presence. So the rubrical directions and the actual way in which a service is conducted are proper concerns for the liturgist. Such a concern was taken up by the Alcuin Club in the publication of its series of Manuals, such as Michael Perham's *The Eucharist*, and perhaps in the wake of the present wave of liturgical revision approaching the year 2000, it is an area which the Club could helpfully address again.

The third point which emerges from a reading of the contributions of those whose work is presented in this book is the close relationship between ecclesiology, our understanding of the nature and purpose of the Church, and the ordering of worship. Recent studies in ecclesiology are drawing our attention to the fact that worship is constitutive of the Church. The Eucharist *makes* the Church, and the Church is the primary context of all her acts of worship and pastoral care. So, the true liturgist needs to be rooted in the life of the Church and to reflect with others on the implications of her worshipping life for the wider social context in which she is set. In the fullest sense of the word, then, the liturgist's task is an ecumenical one, in working together with colleagues from other churches, accepting the fact that no one tradition has the monopoly on words and ways of worship and, above all, remembering too the fact that as the liturgical theologian Aidan Kavanagh so graphically put it, the Church doing liturgy is the Church doing world. True worship does not belong to the postmodern ghetto, and neither is it about the participants' making and expression of meaning and feeling (which is a real danger of experimental and so-called alternative worship), but the bringing of creation and the bearing of human lives before the transforming presence of the triunal God.

Finally, one might record the contribution of liturgists to the process of liturgical revision and the drafting of new texts for the Church's worship. A good number of the people discussed in this volume have served on Anglican Liturgical Commissions and helped to shape forms of worship, but as the reader will discover, liturgical revision is a contentious and controversial business, and some of the liturgists portrayed here, Ratcliff and Willis, for example, were injured in the conflict. From the early days of Prayer Book revision in the 1920s the Alcuin Club has sought to stimulate discussion and suggested possible ways to arrive at a successful conclusion. The year 1923 saw the publication of what came to be known as the 'Orange Book', a positive and eirenic survey, drafted by Frere, of the proposals for the envisaged revised Prayer Book. More recently, in 1989 and 1991, the Club published two volumes edited by Michael Perham, *Towards Liturgy 2000* and *Liturgy For A New Century*, with the express intention of initiating and responding to the debate concerning the kind of liturgical provision which might succeed The Alternative Service Book 1980. This debate is largely carried out on the floor of the General Synod, and forms of worship proposed by the Liturgical Commission are subjected to the blue pencils of those of its number who are appointed to revision committees. So, the outcome is not the work of liturgists, but the result of the further revision and debate of those serving on the General Synod. Proposed texts for worship are thus processed through the machinery of church government. Of course, there needs to be wide debate and proper consultation among the wider Church, but one cannot help observing how within a Synod, which in recent years has become increasingly political, proposed texts can be mauled and almost sabotaged in the interests of narrow ecclesiastical party interests and allegiances, but perhaps as Gordon Jeanes comments in his essay on Willis, compromise and politics are ever the business of liturgical authorization.

The people portrayed in this volume of essays were all in their own ways involved in and concerned with liturgical scholarship, the conduct of worship, theology, and liturgical revision. The gallery is comprehensive, though not exclusive, and a number of different theological stances are represented. There are, predictably, Anglo-Catholics such as Couratin, but we also include the modernist, R. D. Richardson, and the radical J. D. Davies, but, again predictably considering our time frame, no Evangelical liturgists appear in the gallery. For this reason it is particularly good to include Phillip Tovey and Bishop Colin Buchanan among the contributors. Bishop Buchanan, a former Principal of St John's College, Nottingham, and member of the Church of England Liturgical Commission, has done and continues to do much to stimulate discussion of liturgical matters in Evangelical circles and to encourage liturgical scholarship and the renewal of worship. Given the ascendancy of the Evangelical wing of the Church of England during the last twenty-five years one could safely predict that if a similar volume to this was published in 2022 the book would include a good number of subjects with an Evangelical background.

It is particularly good to include essays by Ruth Meyers and Michael Moriarty and to record something of Anglican renewal and scholarship in the United States, but the fact remains that the range of subjects written about in this collection does not reflect the present spectrum of Anglican liturgical life worldwide. The community of Anglican liturgists, as constituted in the biennial International Anglican Liturgical Consultation, is vigorous, and reflects the full cultural diversity of the Anglican Communion. Its published papers and recommendations make the liturgical climate of the Church of England appear cautious and conservative. Recent liturgical revisions from New Zealand, Australia and South Africa have been imaginative and have shown a serious attempt to cast liturgical language in appropriate cultural forms.

One might also make the observation that three of the subjects written about here, who exerted the greatest influence upon liturgical renewal and revision in the first fifty years of the twentieth century, namely Frere, Hebert, and Dix, were members of Anglican Religious communities. The days when communities ran large institutions have largely come to an end and, in reviewing their life, some are recapturing their original charism, and organizing their life on a more human, rather than institutional, scale. But whatever communities are called to be, the worship of the Church is always at the heart of their life together. The Archbishop of Canterbury, George Carey, recently described Religious communities as the best kept secret in the Church of England, and perhaps the time has now come for the Church to recognize the distinctive contribution that communities might make to the life and mission of the Church today, and offer more support to them in this period of renewal, actively calling others to consider the possibility of life and ministry within, or in close association with, a Religious community.

This present volume is a necessary reminder of the impressive legacy of liturgical work which has been undertaken by Anglicans, some of whom have been distinguished scholars, others influential writers, but all concerned with worship, the single most potent source for nurturing the Christian spirit and in shaping Christian cultures. Today, although the opportunities for liturgical research and serious academic study of the subject in English theology departments, church colleges, and ordination courses have diminished alarmingly (with currently not a single Anglican University post-holder in the subject), there are signs of positive developments within the wider Anglican liturgical scene and, if nothing else, the essays offered here are a clear testimony to the seriousness with which the Church of England has considered its liturgical heritage and the task of shaping its worship.

1

FRANCIS PROCTER

PHILLIP TOVEY

Francis Procter (1812–1905) is one of the great liturgical commentators of Anglicanism. His *A History of the Book of Common Prayer with a Rationale of its Offices* stood for fifty years as a standard work and then, after being rewritten by W. H. Frere, remained in print for another fifty years. Procter was fellow and tutor of St Catherine's College, Cambridge, from 1842–47, and then became vicar of Witton, in Norfolk, until he died. He was a liturgical scholar, mostly interested in the Book of Common Prayer, but he later studied pre-Reformation English usages which preceded the work of Cranmer.

HISTORY AND RATIONALE OF THE BOOK OF COMMON PRAYER

There is a long tradition of Anglicans writing commentaries on the prayer books they produce. Indeed, this might well be a distinction of Anglicans from the other churches of the Reformation. It began in a somewhat polemical mode with Bucer's *Censura* and Peter Martyr's lost comments, and developed with Cosin's three volumes of *Notes*. However, it was the seventeenth century which saw some classical commentaries, Sparrow's *Rationale*, Nicholl's *Commentary*, Comber's *Companion to the Temple*, and Wheatley's *Rational Illustration*. It was this latter book that was to become a standard commentary on the Prayer Book, going through many editions.

Procter followed the historical method of this Anglican tradition. In many of these works careful attention was given to the historical development of the text of the service. Indeed, the first half of Procter's book is a history of Anglican liturgy, with his detailed comments on the service coming in the second section. This is in contrast with other traditions of liturgical commentary. Germanus, Cabasilas, or Moses bar Kepha, were not interested in the historical development of the service. They used the allegorical method to explain the spiritual realities behind the present rite. Anglican commentators were also interested in spiritual realities, but their approach was historical, looking at the development of the text of their liturgy. There is still today a particular concentration on the words of the text that marks out an Anglican approach.

Procter does not follow the comparative method of Hamon L'Estrange. In the *Alliance of Divine Offices* (1690) L'Estrange collects together the texts of the services that had existed up to his day and puts them in columns, which facilitates understanding how services differ and have developed. This method was to be followed by F. E. Brightman in *The English Rite* and by P. V. Marshall in *Prayer Book Parallels*. It also prefigures collections of texts such as P. J. Jagger's *Christian Initiation 1552–1969*, B. Wigan's *The Liturgy in English*, and C. O. Buchanan volumes *Modern Anglican Liturgies*, *Further Anglican Liturgies*, and *Latest Anglican Liturgies*. Marshall says of L'Estrange that 'he certainly set a minimum standard for liturgiology in England, both in regard to knowledge of ancient texts and the politics and development of the English rite'. However, Procter develops Wheatley more than L'Estrange, not using L'Estrange's comparative textual methods.

Procter acknowledges his debt to Wheatley: 'during the greater part of the past century Wheatley's *Rational Illustration* had been the chief, and very valuable source of knowledge on liturgical questions'. Later Frere was to make similar comments about Procter talking about 'the solidity and value of Mr. Procter's work'. Wheatley carefully comments on the services of the Book of Common Prayer. His introduction is a response to those of his day who were against set forms of prayer. In developing Wheatley's method, Procter divides his book in two. The first half is a 'General History of the Book of Common

Prayer', including the late medieval situation. The second half is the detailed commentary, 'The Sources and Rationale of the Offices'. Thus history has become more influential in Procter than Wheatley, and takes a much greater place in the work of commentary. Indeed, in this schema it becomes a prerequisite to commentary.

Procter's first edition was in 1855. A second edition in 1856 was reprinted six times. The third edition of 1870 was reprinted eleven times, twice with additions. This is a considerable work of revision and rewriting. He explains that his original way was to build on Wheatley, but:

> in the course of the last thirty years the whole subject [liturgical questions] has been investigated by divines of great learning, and with an accuracy of research which has given to the present generation the advantage of trustworthy information . . . it was mainly with a view of epitomizing their extensive publications, and correcting by their help sundry traditional errors, or misconceptions that the present volume was put together.

He particularly points to the work of J. J. Blunt, *The Annotated Book of Common Prayer* edited by J. H. Blunt, and W. M. Campion and W. J. Beaumont, *The Prayer Book Interleaved.* Procter continued revision of his book, developing an interest in the pre-Reformation liturgies as he mentions in his preface of 1880.

W. H. Frere rewrote the work in 1901, forty-six years after the first edition. He explains that 'while the general outline and plan has been retained, the greater part has been rewritten'. Once again it has been further historical and liturgical research that has led to the need for the revision of the book. 'While much, therefore, of the former work has been superseded, and much new matter has been added, very little has been simply omitted.' This is a testimony to the abiding value of Procter's work. Procter and Frere went through another eight editions. This did not stop others from writing commentaries, e.g. C. Neil and J. M. Willoughby, *The Tutorial Prayer Book.* In the 1960s, Evangelicals come onto the scene with a series *The*

Prayer Book Commentaries edited by F. Colquhoun. However, with the liturgical movement the Church of England's attention is now given to new services. Thus commentaries have been written, including the Church of England's Liturgical Commission, *The Alternative Service Book, a Commentary by the Liturgical Commission*; R. Jasper and P. Bradshaw, *A Companion to the Alternative Service Book*; C. Buchanan, *Anglican Worship Today*; and across the Atlantic, M. Hatchett, *Commentary on the American Prayer Book*. Recent liturgical revision in England since 1980 has also received careful comment in the Grove Book Worship Series, and in various volumes edited by M. Perham and K. Stevenson. This change of focus still leaves Procter and Frere as the standard work on the 1662 Prayer Book, even at the end of the century in which it was written.

PROCTER'S LITURGICAL THEOLOGY

Procter expounds a moderate liturgical theology. This can be shown in looking at some of the points of controversy in the Prayer Book and contrasting his approach with other commentators: first, by looking at the absolution in Matins; secondly, by examining the prayer of consecration; thirdly, by investigating 'seeing that this child is regenerate'; fourthly, by reviewing confirmation; finally, by briefly viewing marriage and the visitation of the sick.

In discussing the absolution in Morning Prayer, he sees this as a substitute for private confession and the absolution as 'effectually conveying' divine pardon to the penitent person. He does not, however, follow Wheatley in saying that through the ministry of reconciliation entrusted to him, the priest conveys and seals pardon to the congregation. Nor does he go quite so far as Blunt who makes no distinction between declaratory and other forms of absolution: to 'declare' God's pardon of sinners is to give effect to that pardon.

In discussing the prayer of consecration Procter says that the prayer is written to 'exclude all notions of any physical change . . . but we pray that we may so receive those creatures of God, to partake of that Body and Blood, truly and really, in a sacramental manner'. Frere simply states that 'it is carefully worded so as not to express any special theory of consecration'. He does, however, open up the role of the Holy Spirit. Blunt and Wheatley say that an epiclesis is implicit in the prayer of consecration. Blunt goes so far as to say about 'we receiving these thy creatures of bread and wine' that by God's benediction there is a supernatural re-creation of the elements.

'Seeing that this child is regenerate' has been a point of controversy in the baptism service. Procter talks of 'the declaration of the undoubted salvation of baptized infants' and points to its origin in *The Institution of a Christian Man*. Frere only adds to Procter a statement on 'it is certain by God's Word', saying 'our reformers are intending to speak of that which is revealed – the covenanted mercy of Almighty God'. Blunt sees in these words 'a key to the doctrine of the Church respecting the condition of the baptized'. The older commentators, however, pass over these words. Wheatley talks in passing of regeneration in the waters of baptism. Cosin does not make any direct comment on the phrase but emphasizes both a change in the water ('in baptism, the nature and substance of water doth still remain, and yet it is not bare water; it is changed and made the Sacrament of regeneration'), and the covenant made between God and the child in baptism.

Procter acknowledges that the ancients called any religious ceremony a sacrament. Thus confirmation can be called a sacrament, but he adds that the narrower definition of the catechism allows only two sacraments. Cosin had been much bolder in simply calling confirmation 'this holy Sacrament'. Cosin also longed for the restoration of chrism, but Procter makes no comment on this. His emphasis in discussing confirmation is the admission to full communion, rather than any pneumatological dimension. Frere was to 'correct' this in his rewriting of the book, adding that confirmation conveys the fullness of the gift of the Spirit.

Procter makes no comment on the giving away of the bride, calling marriage 'an holy estate'. Wheatley had said of the giving away that 'the father resigns her up to God, and that it is God, who, by his Priest, now gives her in marriage, and who provides a wife for the man, as he did at first for Adam'. Procter notes that the confession in the visitation of the sick 'contains the medieval indicative clause, dispensing pardon' but points out that this is only in limited circumstances. He does not follow Wheatley in desiring a restoration of the unction of the sick.

From these few quotations we can see Procter as being less interested in advocating change, and interpreting in a moderate vein, when compared for example with Blunt. Wheatley and Cosin have the agendas of their centuries, when liturgical change was in the offing. Procter lived in a time of stability so we do not find him an advocate of revision but a careful expositor of the status quo.

BREVARIUM AND MARTILOGE

Procter interprets the medieval English history to be one of liturgical independence of Rome, saying that Augustine did not impose the Roman rite but gave 'to the English Church its own national Use'. This approach led him in later years to the furtherance of the study of the medieval uses. His first work was in co-editing the Sarum Breviary. He describes the Use of Sarum as 'most remarkable . . . a reformation of the Ritual based on earlier English and Norman customs'. Indeed, he saw the office as that part most independent of Rome. Thus Procter worked with C. Wordsworth to publish in 1868 a new edition of the text of the Breviary.

The Martiloge was another pre-Reformation text. In 1526 an English translation of a martyrology was printed by Wynkyn de Worde. Once again Procter collaborated in producing a reprint of this edition. His role seems to have been correcting this edition against a copy of the Martiloge found in Lincoln.

Both of these works show an interest in wider liturgical fields than the Prayer Book. They also reveal a Catholic approach that is not Romanizing, but one that upholds the freedom of the English church in the ordering of its liturgy. Indeed, the common use of the phrase 'the English Church' and slightly less 'the English Prayer Book' indicates his belief in the liberty of the English church in its liturgical matters, while at the same time his historical approach suggests an importance of the connection of the reformed liturgy with its English roots.

FRANCIS PROCTER: AN ASSESSMENT

Francis Procter wrote one of the standard works on the Book of Common Prayer. This is a part of the great Anglican tradition of liturgical commentary. Indeed, for the English church there are three standard volumes, Wheatley, Procter, and Procter and Frere. It is a great tribute to his work that Frere was willing to use it as the basis of his commentary, thus ensuring that Procter's contribution to English liturgical understanding should influence another century. Today, the Church of England finds itself in the anomalous position of having the Book of Common Prayer as its basis in worship, but having no new commentaries written on the Prayer Book in the past thirty years. There needs to be some encouragement of liturgists to write new Prayer Book commentaries, not least for a new generation of worship leaders for whom 1662 is unfamiliar. Though a parish priest, Procter was able to hold this position and continue with his liturgical writing. It is to be hoped that today's Church of England will arrange space for parish priests to continue in the same tradition.

SELECT BIBLIOGRAPHY

With E. S. Dewick, *The Martiloge in Englysshe*, Henry Bradshaw Society, Vol. III, 1891.

With W. H. Frere, *A New History of the Book of Common Prayer with a Rationale of its Offices*, Macmillan, 1901.

A History of the Book of Common Prayer with a Rationale of its Offices, Macmillan, 1855.

With G. F. Maclean, *An Elementary History of the Book of Common Prayer*, Macmillan, 1868.

With G. F. Maclean, *An Elementary Introduction to the Book of Common Prayer*, Macmillan, 1862.

With C. Wordsworth, *Brevarium ad use Sarum*, Cambridge University Press, 1882.

2

JOHN WORDSWORTH

CHRISTOPHER IRVINE

John Wordsworth (1843–1911) was the great nephew of the romantic poet William Wordsworth and eldest son of Christopher, former Headmaster of Harrow, Bishop of Lincoln, and hymn-writer, whose compositions occupy a place in the canon of classic Anglican hymnody. John was educated at Winchester and New College, Oxford, and in his adult years as a clergyman exemplified the Anglican genius of combining a life of scholarship and pastoral care. After Oxford he taught briefly at Wellington, working under and gaining the trust of Dr Benson, the future Archbishop of Canterbury, and then returned to Oxford as a Fellow of Brasenose; he ended his academic career as the first Oriel Professor of the Interpretation of Scripture, a post he conscientiously combined with a canonry at Rochester cathedral. Wordsworth was a brilliant Latinist and his scholarly reputation was secured with the publication of *Fragments and Specimens of early Latin* (1874). His *magnum opus*, which occupied him from 1878 to 1905, was a critical edition of the Vulgate text of the New Testament. His fine and accurate skills as a Latinist were put to excellent use in the drafting of the Archbishops of Canterbury and York's reply to the Apostolic Bull *Apostolicae Curae* (1896), which had pronounced Anglican orders to be null and void.

John Wordsworth, a loyal son of the Church of England, was convinced of its status as part of the one, holy, catholic, and apostolic Church. He shared his father's antipathy to Rome, and felt sympathetic to the Old Catholic Movement on the Continent. He also had a growing interest in the churches of the East. In 1885 he was nominated to become bishop of the large and rural diocese of Salisbury. Following his father's example in Lincoln, John was assiduous in his pastoral visitations around the diocese and in his oversight and care of the clergy. He insisted that the *jus liturgicum* was invested in the office of bishop, and gravely exercised this particular responsibility. Both his visitation addresses and his letters to the clergy reveal the seriousness with which he regarded the conduct of worship in the churches of his diocese. The directions he gave were categorical and unambiguously stated. Elaborate ceremonial was roundly declared to be distracting, and the use of incense and the practice of reservation was unequivocally banned, but not without explanation. Addressing the subject of reservation, for instance, he carefully set out and compared the various rubrical instructions concerning the orders for the communion of the sick in the English Prayer Books, and explained the practice, attested to by Justin Martyr, of deacons taking communion immediately from a celebration of the Eucharist. Having marshalled what he considered to be the relevant evidence, he then conceded that on both theological and pastoral grounds it might be appropriate for such a practice to be followed at Easter, and at other major festivals, so that the sick would feel themselves to be 'partakers with the whole in a common eucharist'. Undoubtedly some of his expressed views, such as his extreme dislike of evening celebrations of the Eucharist, were firmly set. But generally speaking, liturgical matters were considered and explained to others, especially his clergy, with the scholar's attention to detail. Sometimes these explanations harboured a profound theological insight which was expressed with brilliant clarity. In one letter to his diocesan clergy, for example, he explained how worship was the occasion when Christians were actively drawn into the life and dynamic movement of the Trinity. Worship, he once said, was the humble, but joyous and confident approach of the Body of Christ, endued both in the whole and in part with the Holy Spirit, and led by its unseen High Priest and Head, to the throne of God the Father.

As Bishop of Salisbury, John Wordsworth sought to increase

his clergy's appreciation of the centrality of the Eucharist in the life and worship of the Church, and a number of his visitation addresses set out a systematic treatment of eucharistic faith and practice. These addresses revealed a wide grasp of liturgical history, the eucharistic theology of the early church Fathers, the Reformers and seventeenth-century Anglican divines, as well as the more practical and pastoral concerns, such as the time and frequency of celebration. The notion of memorial emerges from these addresses as a key concept in the eucharistic doctrine he sought to expound. He argued that its roots were to be found in Hebrew thought and cultic practice, and that it was aptly applied to the Communion as the memorial of Christ's saving work. But he insisted that it defied any narrow definition or attempt to say, in any exclusive sense, at which point in the whole celebration the memorial happened. Thus, adopting a predictable middle course, Wordsworth argued that the memorial (the anamnesis of Christ) was more than a bare commemoration, but not a repetition of Calvary. It was, he claimed, between the two – too mysterious to allow too precise a definition. The Communion was the celebration of the holy mysteries, an understanding of which Wordsworth considered to be consonant with the doctrine of the Prayer Book. These holy mysteries were not to be construed in terms of a fixed and localized sacramental presence, but in the dynamic terms of worshippers being caught up with Christ in his offering to the Father. This dynamic view, he observed, was signalled in the *sursum corda* of the opening dialogue of the so-called prayer of consecration. Furthermore, by being thus drawn into this God-ward movement, worshippers were brought to the threshold of mystery, momentarily caught up in the worship of heaven, and silenced by the encounter with the holy God. For Wordsworth, such a lofty view of worship had implications for devotional and ceremonial practice, and in expounding the view, he directed his criticism against Anglo-Catholic ceremonial (which, incidentally, was largely unknown in the diocese of Salisbury) by forcefully drawing the conclusion that there should be no ringing of a bell, or sound of any kind, during or after the prayer of consecration, but a solemn and aweful silence.

Confirmation has become something of a Cinderella in the current climate of liturgical debate, but this was not the case in the time of John Wordsworth. Wordsworth considered confirmation to be the genius of English religion. He argued that its practice was well established in pre-Reformation England, and recognized that despite the accusation of its unscriptural basis made by Wycliffe in England and by the Continental Reformers, the rite survived with Cranmer. Cranmer, however, did share the Reformers' conviction that the young should receive an adequate form of catechesis, and so a form of catechism was bound up with the ceremony as an integral part of the process. Thus, the classic Anglican conception of confirmation, received and promoted by Wordsworth, was that the young, baptized as infants and now informed of the rudiments of Christian belief and practice, confirmed their faith before a bishop, who with the laying on of hands prayed for the strengthening of the candidates by the Holy Spirit. Wordsworth endorsed this view and especially welcomed the opportunity afforded by the practice of episcopal confirmation of visiting parishes and encouraging those who were young in the faith. But the pastoral value of a practice does not in itself justify a liturgical rite, and the current consensus is that the traditional Anglican pattern of baptismal washing, episcopal confirmation and subsequent communicant status, not only represents a dislocated rite, but implies that something more is required than baptism for an individual to be incorporated into the Body of Christ. Like his contemporaries, though, Wordsworth held that confirmation was in some sense a completion of baptism. The problem with this received view is that it begs the question of how and in what way baptism might be deficient. The difficulty is compounded for Anglicans because both the formularies and the articles of religion in the Book of Common Prayer would suggest that although confirmation invariably provided the gateway to Communion, it was not seen as being necessary for salvation. The 1662 Book of Common Prayer designates baptism and Eucharist as the two gospel sacraments and, furthermore, allows those 'desirous to be Confirmed' to receive Communion. With this background it is understandable why confirmation is increasingly being seen as a pastoral rite, particularly a rite in which the Church (presumably symbolized by the presiding bishop) publicly recognizes and commissions those who have received a significant degree of Christian formation to engage actively in Christian service and ministry. Wordsworth might point to a possible solution. On one occasion he described confirmation as being 'ordained to the lay-priesthood', but such language does invite misunderstanding and possible confusion. However, in contemporary debate the view of confirmation as an episcopal commissioning rite for the laity is gaining currency. Locating confirmation as a 'pastoral' or 'episcopal' office neatly removes the rite from the area of initiation, but it is not without its own problems. Two questions immediately present themselves. The first is the question of the appropriate (earliest?) age at which the rite should be celebrated, and the second, arising from the frequent changes in the work and circumstances of the individual in contemporary life, is whether it would need to be a repeatable rite in the life-cycle of the adult Christian. For Wordsworth living in a more stable and structured society, confirmation was regarded as being vindicated by its practice, but today, social changes, the ecumenical context of theology, and liturgical scholarship and revision have conspired to make it a disputed rite.

In terms of liturgical construction, mention must be made of Wordsworth's work in researching and compiling forms for the consecration of churches. He first became interested in the subject in 1886, when he was asked to draw up the service for the consecration of the chapel at Marlborough College. This was regarded as a model of its kind and came to be adopted by a number of dioceses. Later, in 1898, he was invited to consecrate the collegiate church of St George in Jerusalem, and the rite used on that occasion was subsequently published together with a commentary. In composing this rite Wordsworth was guided by seventeenth-century Anglican precedents, such as Bishop Lancelot Andrewes' practice of a stational procession to the different parts of the church building, and Bishop John Cosin's rendering of the *Veni Creator*. Appropriately, as Bishop of Salisbury, Wordsworth used the triple trinitarian greeting of the peace, 'Peace be to this House from God our heavenly Father . . .' from the Sarum form, but the actual prayer of consecration and its preceding litany were drawn from the Greek *Euchologion*.

Other liturgical projects undertaken by Wordsworth included the restructuring and an arrangement of the *Te Deum*, which developed the lines of an earlier article on the canticle, which was published in Julian's *Dictionary of Hymnody* (1892). In terms of scholarship, however, Wordsworth's most significant contribution arose from his lifelong interest in the Coptic Church of Egypt. In 1898 a German scholar, Georg Woddermin, published a Greek manuscript from the library of Laura on Mount Athos, consisting of thirty prayers ascribed to Bishop Sarapion of Thmuis, who was a contemporary of Antony and Athanasius. Wordsworth recognized that the so-called 'Sacramentary of Sarapion' was a liturgical document of great importance, and published an English translation together with a substantial introduction the following year. A revised edition of the volume appeared in 1909. Today, liturgical scholars seeking to establish the origins of Christian worship are looking with increasing interest, despite the paucity of extant material, to the liturgical documents of Egypt and Alexandria, a move wittily described by Maxwell Johnson as an 'exodus in reverse'. Of particular interest in this renewed attention to Egyptian sources is the structure of Sarapion's eucharistic prayer, its distinctive form of *sanctus*, Alexandrian epiclesis, and its neat transitional phrase, playing on the words 'full' and 'fill', which links the *sanctus* and the institution narrative. The Sacramentary of Sarapion is a collection of prayers for the use of a bishop, and includes forms for the blessing of oils, baptism, a prayer for the burial of the dead, and ordination, as well as the Eucharist. But these occur in the manuscript in a fairly random order. In his own rendering and setting out of the prayers, Wordsworth followed the order of prayers as arranged by Woddermin. This arrangement was altered by Brightman, and again more recently by Geoffrey Cuming in an article 'Thmuis Revisited', published in 1980. In the new text for students published by Alcuin Grow in 1993, Barrett-Lennard recorded his indebtedness to Wordsworth's work.

Finally, with the ratification of the *Porvoo Statement* bringing the Anglican churches of the British Isles and the Scandinavian and Baltic churches into full communion, Wordsworth has been rightly remembered and his foundational work celebrated. Following the Lambeth Conference of 1908, Archbishop Randall Davidson invited Wordsworth to chair a committee with the brief to explore further the possibilities of a closer alliance with the Church of Sweden, and to join a delegation which had been invited to Uppsala to spend three days on a fact-finding tour. Wordsworth gladly accepted the task and clearly enthused in Sweden – as one of his fellow delegates, the Evangelical Bishop Herbert Ryle of Winchester, wrote to Archbishop Davidson and expressed his concern that there would be 'difficulties in restraining John Sarum'. On his return, Wordsworth shared his enthusiasm with his diocesan senior staff and expressed the view that he looked for a 'definite form of alliance' between the two churches 'at no distant date'. Invited to give the Hale Lectures in Chicago, in 1910, Wordsworth chose the Church of Sweden as his subject, and the lectures were published the following year. The book was recently acclaimed by Lars Österlin as 'a great and remarkable achievement'. Wordsworth's initial interest in the Church of Sweden sprang from his attachment to the historic episcopate, and in reviewing his various liturgical concerns, it seems as though they all revolved around the episcopal office, reminding us that a bishop is the primary liturgical minister of the Church. The very office demands, therefore, that those who exercise *episcopacy* within the Church of God are, in the fullest sense of the term, liturgically informed.

SELECT BIBLIOGRAPHY

Bishop Sarapion's Prayer-Book, SPCK, 1899.
Fragments and Specimens of Early Latin, Clarendon Press, 1874.
The Holy Communion, Parker, 1861.
The National Church of Sweden, Mowbray, 1911.
On the Rite of Consecration of Churches, SPCK, 1899.
The Te Deum, SPCK, 1902.

3

J. WICKHAM LEGG

MARTIN DUDLEY

'In the March of 1892, I found myself at Arles; and wandering up into the cloister on the south side of the church I found a sculptured figure of St Stephen at the north-east corner where the two walks join.' This is not, as it might easily be, the opening line of one of the 'Ghost Stories of an Antiquary'. It is the beginning of a learned paper by John Wickham Legg (1843–1921), first Chairman of the Alcuin Club, on unusual forms of linen vestments. Legg might well have been a creation of M. R. James or even of Arthur Conan Doyle. Born on 28 December 1843, he studied medicine at University College, London, and held various appointments before becoming Casualty Physician at St Bartholomew's Hospital, Smithfield, in 1870 and Assistant Physician, a senior appointment, in 1878. His standard textbook, *The Examination of Urine*, ran to eight editions. In 1875–76 he received the two fellowships that mark the poles of his professional and scholarly life, first the Fellowship of the Society of Antiquaries, then the Fellowship of the Royal College of Physicians. In 1887, following two bouts of rheumatic fever, he retired from the medical profession and applied himself to his other great interest, liturgy. In the *Dictionary of National Biography*, S. L. Ollard wrote: 'The study of liturgies was a strong interest in his life, and he now had the leisure to bring to it the accurate scientific training which, joined to his brilliance and eagerness for research, had made his reputation as a physician. In his new field of learning he rapidly obtained a European reputation . . .' He was involved from the outset with the Henry Bradshaw Society, founded in 1890 in memory of the librarian of Cambridge University, Henry Bradshaw (1831–86) 'for the purpose of printing liturgical manuscripts and rare editions of service books and illustrative documents, on an historical and scientific basis, preference being given to those which bear upon the history of the Book of Common Prayer or of the Church of England.' He worked indefatigably on the Society's behalf, serving as Chairman of the Council from 1897 and himself editing the *Missale ad usum Ecclesiae Westmonasteriensis* (3 vols, 1891–97); *Missale Romanum 1474* (1899); *The Processional of the Nuns of Chester* (1899); *Three Coronation Orders* (1900); *The Clerk's Book of 1549* (1903); *Tracts on the Mass* (1904); the second recension of *The Quignon Breviary* (1908); *English Orders for Consecrating Churches* (1911). In addition, and not for the Society, he edited the *Breviarum Romanum a Francisco Cardinali Quigonio* (1888); *The Scottish Liturgy* (1899) and, from three early manuscripts, *The Sarum Missal* (1916). By these extraordinary labours he, together with (to quote Vernon Staley's expression) other 'liturgiologists and antiquaries', laid the foundations for the scholarly study of the English liturgy and its antecedents.

Legg's concerns were not, however, merely antiquarian, as is shown by some of his more polemical writing, his role in founding the Alcuin Club, and his opposition to the revision of the Book of Common Prayer. Legg also founded and edited *The English Churchman's Kalendar*, with notes, pictures, liturgical colours, and the lessons which helped, in a very practical way, to establish good practice liturgically. We find Legg in the chair at the inaugural meeting of the Alcuin Club on Tuesday, 12 January 1897, when its object is set forth as that of promoting 'the study of the history and use of the Book of Common Prayer'. The original intentions of the Club's founders, Legg, Briggs, St John Hope, and Micklethwaite, were somewhat enlarged when set out on a page at the rear of Tract 1, J. T. Micklethwaite's *The Ornaments of the Rubric* (1897). It is, however, a precise expression of the Chairman's own position. The existence of the Henry Bradshaw Society, the Plainsong and Medieval Music Society, and St Paul's Ecclesiological Society were acknowledged, but there was 'no Society which dealt with the practical study of ceremonial, or the arrangement of churches, their furniture and ornaments, in accordance with the rubrics of the Book of Common Prayer'. And so the Club was formed to encourage this study which 'although practical, is intended to work upon purely historical, and of course, English lines'. The Club's guiding principle, from Tract 1 onwards, was 'strict obedience to the Book of Common Prayer'. Great care was taken over this first publication, and the Minute Book shows that it was considered at meetings, held that year at Legg's house, 47 Green Street, Park Lane, on 4, 12, 21, 27 May, 4, 9, and 19 June, at which it was finally agreed, though only with an appendix, on the position of altar candles, by some members of the Committee.

At the meeting on 12 January 1898, Legg indicated an intention to resign as Chairman, which he did by a letter dated 19 January. He gives no reasons other than 'recent circumstances'. There is no indication of disagreement and, given his commitment to editing texts for the Henry Bradshaw Society, the extensive demands on Legg's time would provide an adequate reason for his resignation. The Committee resolved to 'accept with great regret the resignation of Dr Wickham Legg, the first Chairman of the Club and desire to express their appreciation of the valuable services rendered by him in the formation of the Club and their hope that it will continue to benefit by his great stores of experience and knowledge'. W. H. Frere proposed the resolution and Athelstan Riley seconded it. Though Legg subsequently applauded much of the Club's work, he never wrote or edited on its behalf.

Legg's opposition to anything contrary to the Prayer Book and his intense dislike of novelties imported from the Continent was supported by his antiquarian research, which he carried on not only in libraries in London and Oxford but also during his frequent travels on the Continent. Whereas the clergy's trips to France and Belgium provided for a constant supply of liturgical novelties, Legg's expeditions took him to places, notably Southern Italy, Sicily, and Spain, where he gathered evidence of pre-Tridentine liturgical practice.

His basic position may be summarized in this way under five headings. First, he held that ancient practices remained in the English Church for more than three hundred years after the Reformation, and attempted to demonstrate this by his extensive, though somewhat selective, study, *English Church Life from the Restoration to the Tractarian Movement considered in some of its neglected or forgotten features* (1914). Legg and other antiquarians were constrained by the Ornaments Rubric. The Rubric required a snapshot of the second year of the reign of King Edward VI. No one had set down at the time what was allowed, and this it was necessary to discover by painstaking research. The major drawback with this position was the way in which it removed liturgical authority from the Church and the bishops to the scholars.

Second, he accused nineteenth-century ritualists of being ignorant of liturgical history and of enthusiastically introducing novelties and un-English ceremonial in direct and deliberate opposition to the Prayer Book and, especially, the Ornaments Rubric. The Oxford Movement did not represent a new beginning in the life of the Church of England, but the heirs of the Tractarians were destroying what still existed in the 1830s and 1840s and foolishly and ignorantly substituting something of lesser antiquity. Legg argues that the eighteenth-century practice, so much despised by the Tractarians, favoured the Edwardine Ornaments but that they had generally fallen into disuse. The clergy create the greatest difficulty for recovery of these traditions, for, he says, it takes a great deal of trouble 'to persuade Clergymen of the Church of England, of all schools, to keep the rules of the Communion of which they are officers'.

Third, even those who acted with good intentions, particularly the ecclesiologists, acted from ignorance because of the undeveloped state of liturgical studies in Victorian times. A clear example of this is the call for medieval ceremonial in churches built or ordered according to the medieval style. 'Medieval', Legg notes, 'is often used to express mere like or dislike. By it some mean what is in their eyes perfect or almost divine; with others it is synonymous with what is weak-minded and contemptible.' But 'medieval' actually covers a period from AD 800 to AD 1500 or later, and within that period there is considerable diversity from the severity and simplicity of the original Roman rite, praised by Edmund Bishop, to the corruptions (as seen by Legg) of much later medieval liturgy. Legg was a member of the Canterbury House of Laymen. He campaigned vigorously against revision of the Prayer Book. His main argument was that among those who would undertake it there were not scholars of such calibre and learning that it would be a worthy revision. Fourth, and closely linked to the third point, he noted the way in which worship was becoming hedonistic. Fifth, against all this he urged faithful obedience to the Ornaments Rubric, as if it was the panacea of all ills, and he berates the bishops for their failure to act.

Many quotations could be used to illustrate these points, but one, in an essay entitled 'Medieval Ceremonial' and written at the turn of the century, expresses Legg's heartfelt contempt for modern tendencies in religion. It has a curiously contemporary ring to it:

> Mr Edmund Bishop, whose prejudices, if he have any, would be on one side, tells us that the genius of the early medieval Roman rite was 'soberness and sense'. The modern extravagance in the use of flower and candles, of theatrical music, the fussiness of modern ceremonial, are all opposed to soberness and sense. If we are to return to medieval services there will have to be a radical change made in the ceremonial adjuncts introduced within the last twenty or thirty years. At the present moment it is no longer authority or precedent that dictates ceremonial. It is mere hedonism – what the parish will like best, or what will draw the largest congregations or what will look the prettiest . . . There can be no doubt that to be in touch with the music-halls is the aim of a great deal of the ceremonial of the day. The wish is to draw people to church; by what means, flower services, egg services, doll services, lantern services, or any other extravagance, does not very much matter; nor what they do when they are got into church. The worship of Almighty God passes into the background.

He had become increasingly pessimistic, for he saw that 'the worst extravagances in ceremonial' were constantly multiplied by copying:

> An 'advanced' church takes up some outlandish trick. Not to be behind the times, it is instantly adopted by another parish, but no one is able to give any reason from authority or precedent for what is done. Its source is imitation. One parish discards altar frontals, or puts lace on its altar linen, lights up seven lamps before the altar, or sets six candles on the altar. At once others begin the same, law and tradition on the subject being left quite ignored. The bishops take no heed of these things; as the idea of making the ornaments rubric an effective test does not seem to have yet established itself in the episcopal mind.

John Wickham Legg died in 1921 and so did not live to see the 1928 debacle which he foresaw. It was better, in his view, to work with what one had than, in trying to change it, open up a whole series of questions that would have been better left unasked.

SELECT BIBLIOGRAPHY

In addition to the various editions published by the Henry Bradshaw Society and *English Church Life* (1914), see the collection *Some Principles and Services of the Prayer Book Historically Considered*, 1899.

Other works, written or edited, include:

An agreement for bringing out the second Quignon Breviary, Henry Bradshaw Society, 1916.

Breviarum Romanum a Francisco Cardinali Quigonio, Cambridge University Press, 1888.

Church Ornaments and the Civil Antecedents, Cambridge University Press, 1917.

The Clerk's Book of 1549, Henry Bradshaw Society, 1903.

The Coronation Order of King James I, 1902.

English Church Life from the Restoration to the Tractarian Movement considered in some of its neglected or forgotten features, Longmans, Green and Company, 1914.

English Orders for Consecrating Churches, Henry Bradshaw Society, 1911.

Missale ad usum Ecclesiae Westmonasteriensis, Henry Bradshaw Society, 3 vols, 1891–97.

Processional of the Nuns of Chester, Henry Bradshaw Society, 1899.
The Quignon Breviary, Henry Bradshaw Society, 1908.
The reformed Breviary of Cardinal Tommasi, SPCK, 1904.
The Sarum Missal, Clarendon Press, 1916.
Three Chapters in recent liturgical research, SPCK, 1903.
Three Coronation Orders, Henry Bradshaw Society, 1900.
Tracts on the Mass, Henry Bradshaw Society, 1904.

4

VERNON STALEY

MARTIN DUDLEY

Born in Rochdale in 1852, Vernon Staley (1852–1933) was prepared for ordination at Chichester Theological College and ordained to the diaconate in 1878 and to the priesthood the following year. His title was served at Hebden, Yorkshire (1878–85). Moving into the Province of Canterbury, he was for ten years chaplain to the Community of St John Baptist at Clewer (1885–95), curate of Ascot, 1895–97, and Vicar of South Ascot, 1897–1901. From there he went to Inverness, as Provost of the Cathedral, 1901–11, and then returned south to be Rector of Ickford in the Diocese of Oxford until his death on 24 September 1933. Staley's handbooks of doctrine and devotion found a ready readership. An effective exponent of the Catholic faith, he also made a significant contribution to liturgical scholarship and practice, not least by editing the many-volumed *Library of Liturgiology and Ecclesiology for English readers*. His legacy is, in almost every respect, that of Wickham Legg. Legg, however, did little to shape English ceremonial in a positive way; he was mostly concerned to show, by antiquarian study, the diversity of medieval practice and the sense of following the discipline of the English Reformers in ceremonial restraint. Staley, the liturgical practitioner, sought to establish the principles of a truly English ceremonial.

Staley's achievement defines a clear opposition to the Western Use school as represented by, for example, Orbis Shipley's *Ritual of the Altar* (1st edn 1871; 2nd, enlarged edn, 1878). The language of the competing schools is initially similar. Shipley claims to be supplementing the English Office of Holy

Communion 'from the source whence it was derived' and with such material 'which has not been distinctly disallowed by the Prayer Book, or some other authoritative document, or which has only been omitted without being prohibited'. Shipley's work was intended 'to graft upon the letter of the English Rite everything from the Uses of Western Christendom, from which it was derived, or with which it is allied, be it devotional or ceremonial, not inconsistent with its temper and spirit'. The ordered and coherent rubrics of the Roman Rite are preferred to the old disorderly Sarum Use – with the claim that in all essentials the Roman and Salisbury liturgies are one – and the customary Use of the Western Church is made the ceremonial authority. Staley set out to demonstrate the erroneousness of this position by scholarly research. In particular, he argues that there is no uniformity of Western usage, no Roman Rite as such, but an enormous diversity embracing the liturgical centres of Rome, Milan, Lyons, Toledo and Seville, as well as the ceremonies, varying considerably from each other, of the Franciscans, the Carthusians, and the Dominicans. National diversity of religious observances and ceremonies is not inconsistent with Catholic principles, and on that basis Staley begins his task.

The Ceremonial of the English Church appeared in 1899 and reached its fourth edition in 1911. It was well received. *The Church Times* observed:

> We require in writers on ceremonial the observance of caution. Mr Vernon Staley conforms to that requirement. He affirms positively nothing which has not been firmly established by research; will have nothing to do with fancy ceremonies; holds fast to the English way of doing things; is thoroughly loyal to the Prayer Book. It is a merit of the book that it could be read with advantage by lay folk, not specially interested in the *minutiae* of ceremonial. What we like about Mr Staley's Book is its adherence to the old ways of the *Ecclesia Anglicana*.

Staley began by establishing why ceremonial was necessary for religion. 'Experience bears witness', he wrote, 'that the employment of religious ceremonies of an appropriate kind is an effectual means of recalling, setting forth, and impressing the great truths of Christianity upon the minds of men.' The polemical nature of his writing is barely disguised by the apparent objectivity; like Legg he was opposed to ritualists of the Western Use school. The key word, therefore, is 'appropriate', but Staley sees the need for something akin to Newman's reserve in the communication of religious truth. Meaning takes precedence over aesthetics.

> Ceremonial actions in divine worship are not performed because they please the eye as graceful and beautiful, but because they mean something. It is very necessary to press this view of ceremonial observances, because, amongst ourselves, the proclamation and acceptance of Catholic truth has not kept pace with the advance of ceremonial.

Ceremonial must be expressive of doctrine already taught and received and it must also be closely related to devotion and morality. 'All outward acts of religion', he argues, 'should proceed from and be linked with, corresponding inward dispositions.' And again, 'the use of external acts of worship, and religious ceremonial generally, is a matter of secondary importance compared with soundness of belief, inner devotion, and moral conduct.'

With these basic principles carefully established Staley turns to ceremonial of an 'appropriate' kind. He does this in the face of, what he considers to be, a great deal of 'inappropriate' ceremonial. Some of it is the result of faulty liturgical knowledge in the 1870s – 'a past age of liturgical knowledge – an age when the knowledge of the science of liturgy among Anglicans was very imperfect and very partial, not to say erroneous in many respects'. Some of it is the result of personal inclination and whim and, in fairly moderate terms, he castigates those who 'follow inclination at the expense of duty, and private sentiment in defiance of authority', for this 'cannot be regarded as desirable'. Obedience to authority is, then, a prerequisite for appropriate religious ceremonial, for, as it is a matter of ecclesiastical order, it is liable to revision by the authority which first imposes it. The Reformation does not, therefore, create a major difficulty;

it is a revision by authority. 'At the Reformation,' Staley boldly declares, 'the English Church retained all the ancient ceremonial which had not been abused by the superstitions of medieval times, necessary and appropriate for the ceremonial expression of the services of the Prayer Book.' He lists the ornaments of church and ministers and the ceremonies that were retained in advance of the most basic argument of the school of liturgiologists and antiquaries that 'the reformed rite may be clothed with the ancient and traditional ceremonies'.

The ceremonial of the English Church is defined by the English Church. In the absence of other authority, appropriate ceremonial is to be established by rigorous historical research and certainly not by reference to foreign authority. Archbishop Benson's 'Lincoln Judgement' was hailed as a great advance for this way of thinking. Staley is able to lay down four principles. The first is a general one: the ceremonial directions of the Book of Common Prayer are to be interpreted 'in the light of the ancient traditions of the whole Catholic Church, and in accordance with the customs which prevailed in England previous to, and at the commencement of, the Reformation'. Second, 'where no new directions were given, the old customs would continue to be followed'. Third, and crucially for much that Staley was trying to achieve, 'omission does not necessarily imply prohibition'. Finally, these principles do not provide general liberty but permission 'to supply what is necessary or desirable for the due performance of the rites contained in the Prayer Book, from ancient and authoritative English sources'.

Shipley had appealed to the ornaments allowed by the rubric, using a list drawn from the *Kalendar of the English Church* (1877). Staley sets down another list, and there is remarkably little in common between them. Shipley lists, in addition to other things, the requisites of eucharistic reservation, exposition and benediction, all eschewed by Staley. The Ornaments Rubric was the battlefield for opponents of all ritual practices and for the advocates of different approaches to ceremonial. Staley sees it as a means of seeing off the advocates of the Western Use for, he maintains, one point admits of no dispute 'namely, that the rubric is so worded as to exclude implicitly any appeal to the usages of any foreign Church whatever, in regard to the ornaments either of the church or of the ministers'.

Staley's *Studies in Ceremonial: Essays Illustrative of English Ceremonial* (1901) was prepared with the help of Wickham Legg and of F. C. Eeles, also of the Alcuin Club. It is, according to the preface, a full, scientific and historical investigation of certain ornaments and ceremonies introduced since 1850 without 'adequate authority'. The essays, eleven in all, range from a consideration of genuflection to a damning report of the biretta. The genuflection chapter is a model of polemical scholarship. It establishes the essential point for the antiquarians that pre-Reformation English ceremonial is not identical with that of the modern Roman Church before demonstrating that there is no English missal that can be used to testify to genuflection. It is, anyway, an accompaniment to elevation, which was forbidden in 1549. He concludes that in England genuflection is now, as it ever has been, unauthorized, and that inclination, or bowing, is the Catholic custom. There is some pretence at scholarship in the final essay but the conclusion is foregone: 'The use of the Italian biretta, as certain English clergy have introduced it, is not only use of an illegal kind of ornament, but it is an illegal use also – the introduction of a ceremony of modern Roman growth.' Staley even goes so far as to cite the prohibition, in Canon 18 of 1604, on men covering their heads in church or chapel in the time of divine service, so as to reiterate the point that 'the wearing of the Italian biretta in church is thus implicitly forbidden by the English Church'. Note, however, that he did not cite it earlier when considering the wearing of mitres!

There are two main limitations in Staley's approach. The primary problem is the way that determination of ceremonial depends upon scholarly research, thus making the antiquarians the arbiters of practice. Against this, advocates of the Western Use put up the witness and authority of a living Church and the advocates of Prayer Book revision put forward the Church of England's rite to determine its own liturgical practice. The other limitation was the inability to respond to religious need by providing for the liturgical seasons. In 1539, Henry VIII commanded the retention of the ceremonies of Candlemas, Ash Wednesday, Palm Sunday and Good Friday, and, in due course, instruction was given for the explanation of their significance. In 1548, these ceremonies were effectively abolished. Staley is careful to point out that the royal proclamation authorized 'the omission of the use' of candles, ashes, palms, etc. The historians of the Ornaments Rubric saw the regnal year from 29 January 1548 to 27 January 1549 as the 'second year of King Edward the Sixth' and, because the ceremonies were already omitted, had to argue that the royal proclamation, emanating in an irregular fashion from the Court party, was not issued 'by authority of Parliament'. Though this argument opened up the possibility of reintroducing the ceremonies, it could not be said to involve a straightforward interpretation of the Rubric. Eager to reintroduce the ceremonies, Staley and others were reading history in the way they wanted it to be read and this placed the integrity of the whole English Use position at risk. Ultimately, the position could not be maintained; 1548 could not dictate the liturgy and ornaments of the twentieth-century Church. In general, the proponents of the English Use supported the 1928 Prayer Book. Its failure also signalled the end of the dominance of liturgiologists and antiquarians.

SELECT BIBLIOGRAPHY

The Ceremonial of the English Church, Mowbray, 1st edn 1899, 4th edn 1911.

Liturgical Studies, Longmans, Green and Company, 1907 (collected essays and articles previously published).

Studies in Ceremonial: Essays Illustrative of English Ceremonial, Mowbray, 1901.

5

F. E. BRIGHTMAN

BRIDGET NICHOLS

Frank Edward Brightman was born on 18 June 1856, into the family of a successful Bristol boot and shoe manufacturer. The household eventually numbered three boys and two girls. Brightman was the second son. According to census information, his two brothers followed their father into the family trade. Frank took a different course, going up to University College Oxford from Bristol Grammar School in 1875. Already he had encountered the Anglo-Catholic Revival at St Raphael's, Bristol, and All Saints, Clifton, and had been both intellectually and spiritually won over. This was to shape his contribution to debates on liturgical reform in the future.

His undergraduate career was not particularly distinguished, except for a first in mathematical moderations. It was after taking his degree that he won the Denyer and Johnson Scholarship and applied himself to gaining a competent knowledge of Hebrew as he prepared to win the Senior Hall-Houghton Septuagint Prize. In September 1884, he entered Ripon College, Cuddesdon, and was ordained deacon by the Bishop of Oxford on 21 September 1884. His ordination to the priesthood followed on 20 December 1885. He returned immediately to Oxford and took up his liturgical studies in earnest at Pusey House, Charles Gore having nominated him as one of its first priest-librarians. Thereafter, except for the year he spent as curate at St John the Divine, Kennington in 1887, he remained in Oxford all his life.

Brightman's time at Pusey House ended when he was elected to a tutorial Fellowship at Magdalen College in 1902. Here he lived for the next thirty years, serving for a brief period as Dean of Divinity. Although he compiled a book of intercessions for the chapel, this has not turned up amongst archive material. It was also in 1902 that he received the only honour ever accorded him by the Church, when the Bishop of Lincoln, Edward King, whom he venerated, made him a prebendary of Lincoln Minster. Academic recognition was to come in 1909 in the shape of an honorary doctorate from the University of Louvain, and Durham University granted him an honorary doctorate in 1914. It is probably characteristic of Brightman that he assisted with the reconstruction of the library at Louvain after the 1914–18 War. From 1911, successive Bishops of Oxford relied on him as their examining chaplain, and from 1923 he was honorary chaplain to his friend Arthur Headlam, Bishop of Gloucester. In 1926 he was elected a Fellow of the British Academy.

It would be easy to misrepresent Brightman as a reclusive don, remembered only for two weighty editions of liturgical texts. Any letters and papers which survived him seem to have been lost or destroyed. He never married, and all but a few of those who knew him personally have died. We have to rely on obituaries, brief references in the biographies of contemporaries, the prefaces to his two substantial works, and the lucid insights and sometimes acerbic opinions of his shorter articles and scattered correspondence for glimpses of personality. The scholar acclaimed by his friend and colleague Darwell Stone as 'the most learned of living liturgiologists' is less elusive: he is present in the perfectionism of his editorial work, his single-minded quests for sources, and in the honesty of his judgements on liturgical matters.

Brightman's entry in the *Dictionary of National Biography* points out that his interest in oriental liturgies was unusual in an age preoccupied chiefly with Latin liturgies. In preparation for his new edition of C. E. Hammond's *Liturgies Eastern and Western* (LEW) he undertook extensive journeys in the Mediterranean and the Middle East and gained an astonishing first-hand knowledge of ancient liturgical texts. A charming anecdote from one of his obituarists, G. A. Cooke, who travelled with him in Egypt and Palestine, recalls Brightman travelling with the proofs of LEW so that any details of current usage could be included. The Archbishop of the Jordan himself rode down from Olivet on a donkey to check the Greek accents in the rites. That his travels gave him an abiding love of the Holy Land emerges in a letter to Bishop Wordsworth of Salisbury in 1897, asking him to 'kiss all the stones of the Holy City for me' on his forthcoming visit to Jerusalem.

Brightman was also extraordinarily conversant with the best scholarly resources of his own day. The footnotes to LEW vol. I and *The English Rite* bear testimony to this, while his occasional 'Chronicle of Liturgica' in the *Journal of Theological Studies*, which he edited with J. F. Bethune-Baker from 1904 until his death, show that he kept abreast of a vast array of newly published material in several modern languages.

By the time of Leo XIII's Bull *Apostolicae Curae* (1896), he was a known authority on ecclesiastical and liturgical history. The Archbishops of Canterbury and York drew on his expertise in drafting their response, and he himself had published a pamphlet on Anglican orders in 1895. Again, as the question of Prayer Book reform gained in urgency, especially after the findings of the Royal Commission on Ecclesiastical Discipline in 1906, his opinion counted. In 1906 he was in favour of reform, unlike many other Anglo-Catholics and members of the English Church Union (he was chairman of the Oxford Branch for many years), though this gave way to greater conservatism later on. When the Advisory Committee on Liturgical Questions was formed in 1912, he was invited to be part of it. His contributions were often felt to be of the nature of objections rather than constructive advances, yet this was in keeping with his meticulous regard for accuracy and good liturgical language. Always, his position was marked by integrity. In a letter to Claude Jenkins, chaplain at Lambeth Palace, about draft revisions in 1915, he was open about his love of the 1549 rite, but equally convinced that the revisers 'ought to sacrifice much to retain the simple fact that at the altar we all say the same thing'. He realized that the Evangelical wing was intractable and made it a statement of policy 'not to give in to them'. We must read this, however, in the light of what follows: 'not [to give in to them] in the way of depriving them of any liberty which the Book allows them, but in the way of refusing any change which deprives us of the like liberty or any language which is not wholly as generous as that of the Book as it stands'.

His remarks on the draft revisions of the National Assembly (NA 84) and the Houses of Clergy (CA 158) and Laity (CA 169), printed in one volume in 1925, are also revealing. He is impatient of fussy wording, indignant over misrepresentations or wilful manipulations of doctrine, and oddly quarrelsome on the subject of church music. It is hard to convey the substance of his reactions fairly without detailed quotation. Suffice it to say that both in their seriousness and in their wit, they anticipate the famous article in the *Church Quarterly Review* of 1927 which found so much fault with the proposed Book of Common Prayer.

Brightman was uniquely equipped to scrutinize efforts at Prayer Book reform. His *English Rite* is witness of this, though W. H. Frere, in his obituary, maintained that this work was not closest to the author's heart: 'All that labour compressed into two thick volumes was given to making sure of the foundations upon which any revision must be built. The result is a fine piece of work, but it was sad that Brightman was diverted to it from other occupations.' What might these 'other occupations' have been? His first loves seem to have been the study of Eastern liturgies and the work of the seventeenth-century Anglican divines, especially Lancelot Andrewes. H. N. Bate, later Dean of York, maintained in his obituary that Brightman's edition of Andrewes' *Preces Privatae* was 'most characteristic of his mind and method . . . [T]he Introduction and Notes which he added are also perfect, alike in accurate scholarship and in the light which they throw upon the faith and mind of Andrewes and upon those of the editor who resembled him so closely.' Yet Bate suggests elsewhere that it was Brightman's choice *not* to devote himself to his own scholarly interests, especially in the last twenty years of his life. Had he done so, 'a great treasure of knowledge now irretrievably lost would have been made available'. One thinks immediately of the collection of Latin liturgies which should have appeared as the second volume of

LEW, though Frere felt that Brightman abandoned a task which could never have been completed to his exacting standards. Instead, he gave his efforts unstintingly to the editorship of the *Journal of Theological Studies*. Visitors to his rooms in Magdalen were confronted by piles of proofs on every available surface, and there is reference in nearly all the obituaries to the amount of time he spent on the work of other authors. This is corroborated by the tributes paid him in the books published by a number of his contemporaries.

We gain only hints of the private side of Brightman from the available sources. His love of children and ability to communicate easily with them crops up several times. Related to this was his love of children's mechanical toys, and his collection grew with successive journeys abroad. Visitors to Oxford could expect demonstrations of new additions as well as impassioned liturgical conversations. It is probably not surprising that his light reading consisted of detective stories. He himself was in some ways a tireless liturgical detective, who never stopped short of denouncing the literary and doctrinal offences of his contemporaries when he found them out. Yet this in no way lessened the regard and affection that he commanded from those who knew him – with the exception of the Roman Catholic liturgist, Edmund Bishop. Brightman and Bishop seem to have sparred with each other over a number of years, and it would a take a longer study than this to analyse the conflict.

A keen interest in ecclesiastical dress marched hand in hand with his formidable command of ritual. Bate recalls a bishop who was not happy that his vestments were correct until Brightman had cut out the pattern in brown paper. Then there was the matter of caps for the bishops, to be worn at the Coronation in 1911. He wrote sternly to Archbishop Davidson on the subject of some supposedly sixteenth-century caps made for the last Coronation. He found these 'merely hideous' and unlike any genuine Tudor or Stuart headgear. 'It would be quite easy', he assured Davidson, 'to have a real Tudor or Stuart cap made, which would be historically right and aesthetically presentable.'

First meetings with Brightman gave the overwhelming

impression of a man 'almost formidably small', completely bald, and softly spoken, though with 'piercing eyes' and capable of great excitement on subjects of interest to him. It was a notable discovery when, on the installation of a microphone system in Magdalen chapel, his voice was found to be better suited to it than anybody's.

We will leave him here in the chapel. For despite the slender resources for a detailed portrait of Brightman, such material as there is suggests that the life which ended on 31 March 1932 almost perfectly integrated the elements of priesthood, scholarship, and humanity. Bate's obituary in the *Lincoln Diocesan Magazine* sums it up:

> He knew all that was worth knowing of Christian rites; but for him knowledge was not the end. He was most himself when he lost himself, as a priest at the altar. There the quiet voice became almost a murmur, and the whole man was absorbed in the great action, to the study of which he had given his life.

SELECT BIBLIOGRAPHY

Books

The English Rite (2 vols.), Rivington, 1915.

Liturgies Eastern and Western, vol. I, *Eastern Liturgies*, Clarendon Press, 1896.

The Manual of the Sick of Lancelot Andrewes, Rivington, 1909.

The Preces Privatae of Lancelot Andrewes, Bishop of Winchester, Methuen, 1903.

Pamphlets

What Objections Have Been Made to Anglican Orders?, Church Historical Society Tract VI, 1895.

Major Articles

'Common Prayer', *JTS* X (1908–9), pp. 497ff.

'The New Prayer Book Examined', *Church Quarterly Review* CCVIII (1927), pp. 219–52.

'The Quartodeciman Question', *JTS* XXV (1923–24), pp. 254ff.

'The Sacramentary of Seraphion of Thmuis', *JTS* I (1899–1900), pp. 88ff. and 247ff.
'The Terms of Communion' in H. B. Swete (ed.) *Essays on the Early History of the Church and the Ministry*, Macmillan, 1918.
Best known entries in S. L. Ollard (ed.), *A Dictionary of English Church History*, Mowbray, 1912:
'Common Prayer, Book of'
'Marriage of the Clergy'
'King, Edward (1829–1910) Bishop of Lincoln'

6

F. E. WARREN

GORDON JEANES

In 1538 German ambassadors had come to England to discuss a possible theological and political alliance. Few of the English bishops were impressed with the idea of a Lutheran-style Reformation, and Richard Sampson, bishop of Chichester, later recounted how the bishops of Durham (Cuthbert Tunstall), London (John Stokesley) and Winchester (Stephen Gardiner) were supplying their theological armoury:

> [My Lord of Durham] hath an old book in Greek, and in that book are diverse things of the old usages and traditions of the old Church; the which diverse times he carried with him to Lambeth: and as I went with him in his barge, he would tell me of diverse places there written for that purpose, and of diverse things then used and ordained by the Greek Church, which were then in controversy . . . These Greek books were sought out only for that purpose, to set forth the old usages and traditions of the Church: because they were thought of authority; and so thought I then very much, I trust well remembered. My Lord of Durham will not say otherwise, but that he and my late Lord of London were fully bent to maintain as many of the old usages and traditions as they might; and so they said it was necessary to do; especially when they appeared by the Greek Church. (J. Strype (ed.), *Ecclesiastical Memorials* vol. 1, part 2, Clarendon Press, Oxford, 1822, pp. 381–2.)

At the time, an appeal to the tradition of the Western Church might have seemed like an acknowledgement of the authority of the Pope. So for Catholic theology or customs, it was necessary to look elsewhere. The Greek Orthodox Church offered a vision of a Catholicism which was not tainted with Popery.

The principle did not change over the years. The quest remained, at various times neglected or taken up, to discover a Catholicism which was not Roman. In the nineteenth century, F. E. Warren was an important figure in this quest.

Frederick Edward Warren was born on 10 November 1842. He was a scholar at St John's College, Oxford, studying Litterae Humaniores, and was later a Fellow of the College. In 1877 he became Vice President and in 1880 Junior Proctor. In 1882 he married, and afterwards served in a number of College livings until his retirement in 1922. He died on 20 December 1930.

Warren was first and foremost engaged in making available to the scholar and the general reader service books which would support the Church of England as a separate and independent Catholic Church. His first publication in this regard was a translation of the Offices of the Old Catholic Prayer Book, issued only a year after the German original was published in Bonn in 1875. Not only would this encourage English knowledge of the Old Catholic Church in Germany, recently formed in reaction to the First Vatican Council, but also it served to reinforce a sense of unity and catholicity among the non-Papal episcopal Churches. The translation includes a detailed comparison with the Roman Catholic originals, and Warren's Preface includes six points in which the Old Catholic Ritual resembles the work of the English Reformers who had drawn up the first English Book of Common Prayer in 1549. The first of these was, 'An adherence, in all essential points, to the ancient formularies of the Catholic Church'. And the last was a slightly cheeky but still very serious claim, against the contemporary uniformity of the Roman Catholic Church, to be working in the spirit of the instructions of Pope Gregory the Great to Augustine of Canterbury, that he was not to impose the rite of the city of Rome but was to adopt whatever was most pleasing to God, whatever its origin.

The next two decades saw the greater part of Warren's scholarly work. His main contribution was his critical editions of the Corpus Christi Irish Missal, the Leofric Missal and the Bangor Antiphonary. His *Liturgy and Ritual of the Celtic Church* included editions of some important texts, in particular the Stowe Missal, and with its many observations on the life and worship of the Celtic Church was still important enough to have been reprinted in 1987.

In all these works, Warren showed the same interests as he had done in his translation of the Old Catholic Ritual. He was concerned to show the catholicity of the Church of England independent of the Papacy. This was set out in a sermon he preached and had published in 1883: *The Autonomy of National Churches not Inconsistent with the Unity of Christendom.* In this work he effectively pre-empted the later phrase coming out of the Roman Catholic–Anglican conversations at Malines: 'united, not absorbed'. Looking towards unification of the divided denominations (none named, but probably the two just mentioned), he waxed lyrical on Papal interference in medieval England, especially from the time of the Norman invasion, and defended the right of a national church to appoint her own clergy as she sees fit, to canonize her own saints, to have her own rules and canons, and her own ecclesiastical tribunals, subject only to the General Council of a re-united Christendom. And of liturgy Warren said:

> Another note of autonomy is the right of a National Church to draw up and use its own form of Liturgy. Uniformity is the rule of modern Rome; variety was the rule of early Christendom. The early Western Churches of Gaul, Spain, Milan and the British islands had their own liturgies. The ancient Eastern Churches of Syria, Constantinople, Egypt, Armenia, etc., likewise had their own liturgies composed and still preserved in the ancient vernacular languages of those countries. The Church of Rome herself was originally a Greek speaking community, and must have possessed a Greek liturgy, which she exchanged at some unknown but early date for the Latin service of later days. Thus, in drawing up her vernacular

> liturgy in the sixteenth century, the English Church certainly took an important step, yet one which it was quite within the competence of a National Church to take.

The Celtic Church was important because it offered the Church of England her own heritage independent of Rome. In the sixteenth century, Archbishop Parker had developed this argument, and now Warren was continuing it with his own research. Jane Stevenson warns us against his view of the Celtic Church, that it implied an ethnic, linguistic and ecclesiastical unity of the Celtic peoples which modern scholars would doubt. Warren was dependent almost entirely on Irish sources, and there are few facts about the Church in Britain. Stevenson goes so far as to describe his approach as 'unhistorical and controversialist'. Especially questionable was his attempt to trace the sources of British worship back, through southern Gaul, to Ephesus. In effect, any source but Rome!

The critical edition of the Leofric Missal was an attempt to identify what freedom and independence the Church in Britain enjoyed on the eve of the Norman invasion. It must be said that the differences between English and Roman use are few and not greatly significant. Indeed, the greater part of the Missal is a standard Gallican version of the Papal Gregorian Sacramentary, brought by Leofric himself to Exeter from the Continent.

Towards the end of his publishing career Warren was still translating: the two volumes of the Sarum Missal appeared in 1911. This work in the series of the Library of Liturgiology and Ecclesiology would have appealed to the followers of Percy Dearmer, who was emphasizing the continuity of the Prayer Book with its medieval roots. The appeal to the past, whether Prayer Book or earlier, earned for Dearmer's work the nickname of 'the British Museum rite', but Dearmer was no mere antiquarian, and Warren likewise was engaged in an attempt not merely to investigate historical detail but to give the Catholic Church of England firm historical foundations for its confident theological claims.

Also in the popular sphere, his *Prayer Book Commentary for*

Teachers and Students continued the theme of his preface to the Old Catholic Ritual: the English Prayer Book of 1549 was presented as essentially a translation: this was 'quite within the competence of a National Church'. Four chief advantages of 1549 were listed: the use of the vernacular; communion in both kinds; the prominence of the Eucharist as a Communion feast; and the removal of medieval additions. No deficits are noted. Earlier, Warren had tried to blame the explicit Protestant theology of the Second Prayer Book of 1552 on 'a multitude of foreign refugees'. Bucer and John à Lasco were named. But even then the most substantial theological change cited was in the words of administration of the communion. When he went on to discuss the text of the Holy Communion, Warren emphasized Mozarabic and Oriental influence on the prayer of consecration. Lutheran forms or Receptionist theology are nowhere suggested.

It is not as if he knew no better. On 24 April 1901 Warren had written to the *Guardian* newspaper a note about the origin of the phrase in the Communion Service, 'these thy creatures of bread and wine'. (It was an embarrassment to a member of the extreme temperance party.) After discussing scriptural and Catholic antecedents, he could not resist a final swipe of *odium theologicum*: 'Let this derivation stand until Messrs Gasquet and Bishop, or others, shall have unearthed an alternative derivation from some Lutheran Ordo.' Of course, it was no time before this challenge had reached the ears of the Roman Catholic liturgist, and Mr Bishop produced a good antecedent from a Lutheran Ordo. Mr Warren was bloodied but unbowed, others offered their thoughts, and the anxiety of the member of the extreme temperance party was forgotten. The identity of the Church of England was at stake, for her theology was to be identified by that of her liturgy, and her liturgy could be determined (so it was thought) by its sources. But Warren's confident parading of Catholic sources to the exclusion of Protestant ones was more polemical than scholarly. One can only admire the confidence with which he attempted it.

This chapter seems to have become a list of criticisms of Warren's scholarly ability. Yet he was no mean scholar, and indeed he was awarded an honorary doctorate of divinity by the University of St Andrew's in 1913. His pure scholarly work is best seen in his critical editions, most of which are still definitive and sit confidently on the University library shelves. But his studies of the early and Celtic liturgies, his approach to the Prayer Book, are marked less by the careful scholar and more by the polemicist who knows all the facts of the case but is concerned only to marshal and present those favourable to his or her cause. Here we have an outstanding example, but in principle is any scholar different, or any scholarship impartial? The contemporary interest in Celtic Christianity is, with some eminent exceptions, no more historical than a century ago. And the current interest in the diversity of early Christian doctrine and worship (I speak of the general fashion rather than any individual writer) is largely a projection onto history of the acceptance of diversity in the modern Church, just as Warren projected onto the facts a separate and independent Catholic Church of England, and others again looked into the same deep well and saw only their reflections.

Warren's vision was perhaps limited, but of his own time he was a shrewd observer. Like scholarly failings, some things in the ecumenical scene never change, and in his sermon on the Autonomy of National Churches Warren could put his case for the Church of England in defiant terms:

> Let those sanguine Roman Catholics and Anglo-Catholics who fancy that they see any hopes of a re-union of Western Christendom, by a general return of the English people or the English Church to the Roman obedience, in its unmodified form, be assured of this, that though here and there from exceptional causes individuals may desert the Anglican for the Roman communion (and *vice versa*), yet that too deep an alienation has been created in English life and feeling by the above named facts and by other causes, to render the idea of a re-union of Christendom by the re-submission of the English Church and people to the claims of Roman supremacy anything more than a baseless chimera and an unsubstantiated dream.

SELECT BIBLIOGRAPHY

The Antiphonary of Bangor, Henry Bradshaw Society, vol. 4, Harrison & Sons, 1893.

The Autonomy of National Churches not inconsistent with the Unity of Christendom: a Sermon, Parker, 1883.

The Book of Common Prayer with Commentary for Teachers and Students, 1905, 2nd edn, SPCK, 1910.

The Leofric Missal, Clarendon Press, 1883.

The Liturgy and Ritual of the Ante-Nicene Church, London, 1897, 2nd edn, SPCK, 1912.

The Liturgy and Ritual of the Celtic Church, Oxford 1881, reissued in 1987 with an Introduction by Jane Stevenson and a Foreword by Henry Chadwick giving historical details, Boydell Press, 1987.

The Manuscript Irish Missal belonging to Corpus Christi College, Oxford, Pickering, 1879.

The Offices of the Old Catholic Prayer-Book, Parker, 1876.

Sarum Missal in English, Library of Liturgiology and Ecclesiology, De la More Press, 1911.

7

WALTER FRERE

ANNE DAWTRY

In his preface to the Alcuin Club edition of Frere's *Correspondence on Liturgical Revision and Reconstruction* Father Bernard Horner, a younger contemporary of Frere's at Mirfield wrote:

> It was impossible to live with Walter Frere without being impressed by the fact that what he really lived for was worship . . . He strove to make his whole life an act of worship. At church, in the study, at recreation and at meals, Frere was always the essential worshipper.

For Walter Frere (1863–1938), life was worship and worship life. Whatever he did, as a student, as an administrator (Frere was superior of the Community of the Resurrection at Mirfield from 1902 to 1913 and from 1916 to 1922), as a bishop and as a liturgical scholar and revisionist, Frere did it to the best of his ability as an offering to God.

Yet within this broad spectrum of worship Frere's own personal spiritual focus was essentially eucharistic. Father Horner tells how at the very end of Frere's life, when he could only shuffle along the corridor to an improvised chapel, he would say: 'This is just what I long for; this is meat and drink to me.' It is hardly surprising then that from his early years as a priest Frere should have had a vision of the Eucharist rather than Matins being the main Sunday Service at least in Anglo-Catholic churches. To this end he established a 9.30 a.m. Parish Communion at St Faiths in Stepney in 1892.

Frere was essentially a holy man. Yet he was also much more. He was a brilliant academic. Having obtained a First Class

Honours Degree in the Classics Tripos at Cambridge he went to Wells Theological College in 1886 where he was described by the then Principal E. C. Gibson as 'the most brilliant and polished scholar whom I have ever trained'. His greatest loves were church history and ancient liturgical texts, and he wrote widely on both subjects. His earliest works include editions of the *Sarum Gradual* and *Winchester Troper* (both published in 1894) and two volumes on the *Use of Sarum* published in 1898 and 1901 respectively. His most famous work is perhaps his complete revision and rewriting of Procter's *New History of the Book of Common Prayer* published in 1902. Yet Frere's academic interests were never esoteric. For him the study of ancient texts had a practical purpose in that it informed the current liturgical debate.

Walter Frere was not only an academic but also a communicator. Throughout all the years of his involvement as a member of the Advisory Committee on Liturgical Affairs to Convocation patience was his watchword and he never tried to impose his opinions on others by force. He always tried to respect his opponent's point of view and was bitterly disappointed when the same courtesy was not returned. As he complained in a letter to the Bishop of Pretoria concerning the 1928 debate in Convocation on the Prayer Book: 'the spirit of generosity has faded and has been replaced by a general desire to tie up everyone who is regarded as tiresome; that is to say the Anglo-Catholics.' Frere was always sensitive to the fact that matters of liturgical revision, and indeed the whole question of religious ceremonial, had a special faculty for stirring up strong feeling in the breasts of those who were at other times quite peaceable:

> From time to time the outside world is surprised and perhaps amused at some sudden outburst of emotion from this source. Bitter attacks, followed by sarcastic recriminations are heard on the cut and colour of clerical vestments, and popular feeling runs high about the positions and movements of those who take part in a service. The excitement seems quite disproportionate to the source . . .

> Moreover these eruptions are more inexplicable than those of an earthquake.

In all arguments on points of liturgy Frere kept his head, and his rich sense of humour often stood him in good stead when called upon to defuse a particularly heated altercation in the Advisory Committee or in Convocation.

Frere himself was a passionate champion of liturgical reform. Indeed, from the time when he had been a student at Wells he had regarded the whole process of liturgical reform within the Church of England as being long overdue. He elaborated upon this further in his *Principles for Liturgical Reform* published in 1907. Liturgical reform, he argued, should involve not just the Church of England but the wider Church also. Revision, he stressed, should include a long period of authorized experiment in which there would be opportunities for education and for further enrichment of the proposed texts. Moreover he believed that such revision should involve not a mere tinkering with texts but a thorough overhaul of the whole Prayer Book undertaken under the guidance of skilled hands. The Book of Common Prayer as it stood was, Frere argued, out of touch with the people. The Church must therefore face local and unauthorized revisions which would be detrimental in the long run, or else make haste to put into motion some scheme for liturgical reform.

There were many in Convocation who agreed with him, including Archbishop Davidson. Yet the House of Bishops at this time was singularly lacking in the 'skilled hands' that Frere had called for in order to oversee the work of revision. Thus in 1911 Archbishop Davidson decided to appoint an Advisory Committee on Liturgical Affairs who might edit and co-ordinate the proposals on liturgical reform which would ultimately issue from the Convocations. The House of Bishops approved, and the Committee, chaired by Dr Robertson, Bishop of Exeter, first met in 1912. It was an impressive gathering and included amongst its members Bishop Gibson of Gloucester and Bishop Drury of Ripon, Professor H. B. Swete, Brightman, Dearmer and Frere. Yet from the start this Committee worked under certain disadvantages. Its terms of reference were far from clear and it could make no proposals of its own and only 'edit and co-ordinate' the proposals of Convocation. This must have been immensely frustrating for men of the calibre of the liturgical scholars on the Advisory Committee. Frere found it particularly so.

Such frustrations notwithstanding, Frere proved himself to be a valuable 'expert witness' on a number of issues. One problem taxing Convocation was what should be the form and content of the alternative canon or eucharistic prayer proposed for insertion into the Revised Prayer Book. There were divided opinions amongst the bishops and liturgists as to which elements were important within the eucharistic prayer. Did the words of institution stand on their own, or was the whole prayer a necessary part of the consecration of the bread and wine? Frere, with his wide and detailed grasp of liturgical texts argued that the consecration of the bread and wine was effected by giving thanks over them and that this involved not just the words of institution but the whole prayer. He also argued that it was necessary to include within this prayer an *epiclesis* or invocation of the Holy Spirit which would strengthen its trinitarian basis. On this matter there was a great deal of opposition both from the Anglo-Catholics and from the Evangelicals in Convocation, who felt that Frere's proposals detracted from the words of Christ at the institution. Although he was clear where he stood himself on this matter, Frere was anxious to protect those whose views were different from his own, and he fought long and hard for their voice to be heard.

His sense of balance and fairness was also apparent in the part which he took in the deliberations on the reservation of the Sacrament. This subject was again hedged around by objections and difficulties, particularly on the part of those who were afraid that reservation might lead to a growth in superstition. Frere was anxious to allay their fears. Whilst he argued that reservation of the Sacrament was in his opinion essential in order that Holy Communion might always be available to the sick and dying, he made clear that reservation was only to be allowed for the use of the sick and not for the purposes of

Benediction, which had been growing in popularity in many Anglo-Catholic parishes. To ensure that the reserved Sacrament was not misused he suggested that it should be kept in a locked aumbry the key to which was only to be made available to authorized persons.

The advice of the Committee for Liturgical Affairs, and Frere's advice in particular, was also sought on the question of what procedures should be followed if either the bread or the wine proved to be insufficient at a service of Holy Communion. The members of Convocation were themselves divided on this matter. Some argued, following the Orthodox Rite, that no further consecration could be allowed in the Eucharist. If the elements ran out then the receiving of communion by some members of the congregation must be deferred to another day. Others argued that further elements could be consecrated, but only if both bread and wine were consecrated together using the words of institution in their entirety. Yet others were of the opinion that if the wine ran out, or if an accident to the cup occurred, then further wine might be consecrated alone using that part of the words of institution beginning 'After supper he took the cup . . .' This was Frere's own position. In a great deal of lengthy correspondence on this issue he displayed an impressive grasp both of the relevant historical liturgical texts and of the traditions of different churches which might be used as evidence in this matter. He was able therefore to guide with authority both the Advisory Committee and Convocation.

Not all of Frere's suggestions were eventually incorporated into the Book of Common Prayer as submitted to Parliament in 1927 and as revised again in 1928. Some of his arguments lost their force after they had been through the committee stage several times, whilst other ideas were lost in the scramble to redeem something of the proposed Prayer Book after its rejection by Parliament. Frere became worried that the book as it now stood was unworkable. He regarded the compromise put forward in 1928 that reservation was only to be allowed under licence from the bishop to be a retrograde step, whilst he deplored the power given to PCCs in choosing which eucharistic prayer was to be used in their parish as insulting both to the clergy and the bishop. When the Book finally came before Convocation again in 1928 Frere with great sadness felt it necessary to vote against it. Yet displaying his customary generosity of spirit, once the 1928 Prayer Book had been ratified by a majority of dioceses he did make provision for its use in his own diocese of Truro.

Outside his work for the Committee on Liturgical Affairs, Frere showed great interest in the whole campaign for lay involvement in the liturgy. At the Parish Communion which he had established in Stepney he encouraged the laity to communicate on a regular basis, whilst he was also interested in involving the laity more in the services of Matins and Evening Prayer. To this end in 1925 he proposed a thorough revision and reworking of the Psalter. This, he argued, should be rewritten in more rhythmical language in order to facilitate congregational participation in the singing of Anglican chant. He also argued that much of the Psalter was unintelligible and at times disturbing to the ordinary person and that a new revised Psalter should contain only those parts of the whole which could be regarded as edifying. The difficulty here was that his proposals would have involved the omission of fourteen psalms in their entirety and of sixty-six passages from other psalms. His pleas therefore fell on deaf ears and there was no attempt to revise the Psalter within the new Prayer Book proposals put to Convocation. The Psalter remained in its entirety in the 1928 proposed book, although it is interesting to note that years later in the Alternative Service Book 1980 provision was made for omitting some parts of the psalms by 'bracketing' them. Frere also had a vision for the inclusion of the laity in the liturgy of Morning and Evening Prayer, which had hitherto been largely the preserve of the priest and clerk. He suggested that in a service of solemn Matins up to fifty people might be used in reading, in leading the responses and as acolytes, etc.

Walter Frere's work as a liturgical revisionist was not confined to the Church of England. His advice was sought by the Church of Japan (1911–14), by the South African church (1919), by the United Church of Southern India (1928) and by the Church in Ceylon (1932). Frere himself had hoped that the necessary revision of the Prayer Book might first come to fruition in England in order that the overseas dioceses might have an example upon which to base their own work. Yet when liturgical revision in England proved to be so slow and, finally, less than wholly successful, Frere lent what help he could to the Anglican dioceses abroad in their own attempts at revision. He undoubtedly found this quite a freeing experience as many of these churches were much less hedged about by committee structures and by a tendency towards erastianism than was the case in England.

In recognition of the contribution which he had made to the whole process of liturgical revision within the Church of England, Frere was appointed Bishop of Truro in 1923. Yet he never ceased to be a Religious as well and when he resigned his see in 1935 he retired to Mirfield, where he ended his days.

For Frere, liturgical reform was an ongoing process. In his preface to Procter's *New History of the Book of Common Prayer* (1902) Frere had paid tribute to the previous fifty years as a time 'full of enthusiasm for liturgical studies almost without precedent'. Yet just before his death in his last work *The Anaphora: An Eirenical Study in Liturgical History* (1938) Frere could recognize that the whole process of liturgical reform had not lost its impetus but was likely to continue far into the future.

Today, some sixty years after Frere's death, we are still part of that process. Much of what he hoped for has now come to fruition. The Eucharist has become the main Sunday Service in the majority of parishes within the Church of England. There have been, and will continue to be, long periods of authorized experimentation on the liturgy. The whole process of liturgical education both of the clergy and laity has grown apace. Yet what of the spirit of patience and forbearance of which Frere was a shining example in his own age? Are we as members of the Church of England any more tolerant now than were Frere's contemporaries when it comes to listening to those whose opinions on liturgy are perhaps different from our own? Perhaps not. Maybe this is one of Frere's lessons which we have still yet to learn.

SELECT BIBLIOGRAPHY

Frere's works are too numerous to list here in full. A complete list of his writings can be found in Appendix 5 of J. H. Arnold and E. Wyatt (eds.), *Walter Howard Frere: A Collection of His Papers on Liturgical and Historical Subjects*, Alcuin Club Collections 35, 1940.

The Anaphora: An Eirenical Study in Liturgical History, SPCK, 1938.
R. C. D. Jasper (ed.), *Correspondence on Liturgical Revision and Reconstruction*, Alcuin Club Collections 39, 1954.
A New History of the Book of Common Prayer, Macmillan, 1902.
The Principles of Religious Ceremonial, Longmans, Green and Company, 1906.
The Sarum Gradual, Plainsong and Medieval Music Society, 1894.
Some Principles of Liturgical Reform, Murray, 1911.
The Use of Sarum, 2 vols., Cambridge University Press, 1898 and 1901.
The Winchester Troper, Henry Bradshaw Society, 1894.

8

W. PALMER LADD

MICHAEL MORIARTY

The Liturgical Movement in the American Episcopal Church owes its origin to William Palmer Ladd (1870–1941), whose ideas helped revolutionize the church's liturgical consciousness and came to fruition in its current liturgy, the 1979 Book of Common Prayer. Ladd was the first in his Church to see in the Liturgical Movement a means of responding to cultural crisis. By reforming its worship, Ladd argued, the Church could prepare itself to speak credibly to a culture that no longer looked to the Church as a unifying force in society or as a source of wisdom or tradition.

Ladd was dean of Berkeley Divinity School, New Haven, Connecticut, where he taught a generation of church leaders, as Professor of Church History from 1904 to 1918 and as Dean from 1918 to 1941. Ladd's written legacy comprises some eighty essays – witty, candid, impatient with obscurantism and pretence, and passionate for the genuine and relevant – which began appearing in church magazines in 1938. During his final illness, Ladd began collecting his essays into a book, *Prayer Book Interleaves* (1942), because he wanted those 'who have the liturgical destiny of the Church in their hands' to 'seriously consider the facts and ideas' he so urgently argued. The book, a milestone in the history of the Episcopal Liturgical Movement, was reissued in 1957; the Church was only then beginning to realize the full import of Ladd's work.

'Nothing is more important than that the liturgical movement should take the right direction in this country at the present time,' Ladd declared. Given the 'eruption of paganism and barbarism in the World War and since,' said Ladd, the urgent question facing the Church was whether 'the modern world will ever again listen to the gospel of Jesus Christ'. In the face of what he called 'our new polytheism' of commercialism and humanism in America, and fascism, communism, nationalism and totalitarianism in Europe, Ladd argued for the liturgy as a means of recovering the bonds of community centred in God and sacramentalized in the Eucharist.

Ladd's nineteenth-century forerunners in Prayer Book reform, William Augustus Muhlenberg (1796–1877) and William Reed Huntington (1838–1909), had begun to frame the terms of the question of liturgical revision in the Episcopal Church, namely the relation of worship to the circumstances of a changing society. The 1892 and 1928 books showed the Church beginning to respond liturgically to massive immigration, missions to blacks and to native Americans, evangelization of the frontier, urbanization and growth of city slums, and ecumenical relations. Nineteenth-century ritualism had a tangential effect on the formation of the 1892 and 1928 Prayer Books. More significant influences were the stirrings of ecumenical interest, the awakening of the Church to the social gospel and a wider missionary outreach, and contact of Anglican missions with non-Western cultures.

Ladd was the first of his generation of seminary educators to point out the liturgical movement's relation to social justice, ecumenism, and Christian art. Ladd became conversant with the pioneering liturgical scholarship in pre-war Germany through his many friends at the Roman Catholic Benedictine abbey at Maria Laach. Ladd brought to Episcopalians' attention the importance of the work of scholars like Ildefons Herwegen (1874–1946) and Odo Casel (1886–1948) at Maria Laach. He recommended the liturgical publications of St John's Abbey in Collegeville, Minnesota, whose Virgil Michel OSB had introduced the modern Liturgical Movement into the United States in 1926. The Dean also brought A. G. Hebert SSM (1886–1963) and Percy Dearmer (1867–1936), both of whose concern for the social implications of liturgy he admired, to lecture at Berkeley.

Ladd frankly scorned both Anglo-Catholic and Roman Catholic liturgical practice as foundations to build on. He accused both of refusing to face reality by failing to cultivate a living liturgical tradition that arose from and responded to the lived circumstances of contemporary life. Ladd's acid criticisms cut into the prejudices of high, low, and broad church parties alike; he rightly saw that the Liturgical Movement would modify the traditions and usages of all parties and be a unifying influence within his Church. His own temperament combined admiration of the austere piety of the Nonjurors and of John Wesley's love for the people and 'willingness to give and take in the world as it is'. Ladd pleaded with his Church to enter intelligently and wholeheartedly into the Liturgical Movement to carry the renewal begun at the Reformation a step further; 'by adapting our inherited forms of worship to the modern situation,' he said, the church can prepare 'to meet the needs of a generation it has done so much to mislead and to alienate'.

Ladd criticized the shortcomings of the liturgy of his time, the 1928 Prayer Book, and argued the need for General Convention, the Church's triennial governing assembly of laity, priests and bishops, to adapt it to contemporary needs. His genius was that he offered a way for ordinary parishes to find a liturgical renewal for the here and now within the orbit of Prayer Book rubrics liberally interpreted, and of established customs. Only as the Church conserves and constantly reinterprets its past does it become competent to deal in the present with live issues and new problems, he said. Antiquity is a good thing, 'but not too much of it at any time'; excessive devotion to it makes a church 'ineffective, and even a bit ridiculous'. A pragmatic appreciation of the need sometimes to have 'the good sense to disregard precedent' characterized Ladd's attitude of openness of mind, liberality of interpretation and adaptability as ways of keeping within the Catholic tradition.

Ladd regarded reform of the Eucharist as 'the heart of the whole liturgical problem'. Facing an indifferent or hostile world, the Eucharist was where the Church ought to concentrate its energies because that is where it can most plainly communicate the gospel and show its own mind – as the primitive Church did until paganism surrendered. Ladd produced a sample rite of 'The Holy Eucharist Simplified' for study and discussion that reduced the eighteen-page Prayer Book rite to four pages. He even proposed that 'laymen' lead the beginning of the service, the priest going to the altar only at the offertory. Though he did not discuss explicitly a theology of the priesthood of the laity, Ladd adamantly argued that liturgy was 'of, by, and for the people. The wretched medieval idea, sanctioned, alas, to some extent in our Prayer Book, that services are the monopoly of the priest, must be dropped.' Even without a revision of the Prayer Book, Ladd suggested ways to realize the active priestly participation of the people: singing at the Eucharist should be congregational, wardens and vestrymen should assist the priest at the altar, present the oblations, read the lessons, and administer the chalice, and lay leaders might even read the gospel on Christmas Day, for example.

Tradition as well as present need indicated to Ladd that the Eucharist ought to be the chief service every Sunday. Since Episcopalians had inherited a custom of monthly late Communion on the first Sunday of the month, Ladd urged clergy to take it as a starting point for a Parish Eucharist that emphasized the corporate character of eucharistic worship and made 'a strong appeal to many who are sick of individualistic and subjective expressions of religion'. The newly confirmed should make their first communion at this service, 'and it is the proper time for adult baptisms'. Taking a cue from 'our Protestant brethren', the monthly Communion could become a 'dedication service' to Christian work and witness in the world, and the first Sunday of each month a 'rally Sunday'. Social concerns that the liturgy made no provision for – such as the parish's high school graduates, missionaries from the parish, labour disputes, political leaders, the sick and well of the parish – could be brought into relation with the liturgy through special prayers and thanksgivings. Despite the similarity of name, Ladd's Parish Communion had a different origin and spirit from its contemporary English counterpart. Ladd started with the American Prayer Book and worship patterns, and borrowed from Protestant examples as well as the contemporary Liturgical Movement.

Ladd encouraged offertory processions, but compared to Roman Catholic liturgists of the time his attitude towards the practice was cool. Its significance as a symbol of self-offering did not loom large in his writings – possibly because he was mindful that the Scottish-American prayer of consecration encompassed the community's offering of itself and union with one another and with Christ in the heart of the eucharistic action. The problem, Ladd acknowledged, was that 'we seem to have little success in tying . . . [eucharistic self-offering] up with the outgoing Christian life, e.g., with social service or missions'.

Interchurch communion smacked too much of a quick and easy cure for the deep-seated disease of Christian disunity, Ladd felt; ecumenical study and frank confronting of differences would contribute more to mutual understanding and possible unity in the long run. Ladd organized an interdenominational Liturgical League in New Haven in the late 1930s to popularize the Eucharist among young people. The league discussed biblical and ecumenical aspects of the Eucharist as well as its social implications, and even compared Anglican, Roman, Orthodox and various Protestant eucharistic liturgies. Ladd's conviction that the reunion of the churches must centre in the Eucharist, not in questions of the ministry, was an approach that later ecumenical dialogues found to be a fruitful way forward, beginning with the formation of the World Council of Churches in 1948 and its several commissions on ways of worship.

Ladd saw at issue in baptism nothing less than modern Christianity's re-encounter with an alien culture. He was scandalized by practices that denied baptism's social implications, like baptizing privately or as a Sunday School event, and trivialization of the sacrament by 'negligible' baptismal fonts. He wanted the sacrament celebrated so that the whole congregation could witness the admission of new members to its fellowship, and he wanted the ceremony dignified with processions, lights, music and burning of a paschal candle during Eastertide – though the idea of reviving the Easter Vigil or of building baptisteries he dismissed as beyond the pale of possibility. Ladd's thinking on initiation bypassed Anglo-Catholics (who 'while proclaiming sacramental doctrine did little or nothing to restore its proper dignity and status to this all-important sacrament') and 'futile' nineteenth-century Evangelical controversies over baptismal regeneration. Baptism created a distinction between Christians and their culture. 'We may smile' at the idea of demons and exorcism which early Christians associated with baptism, said Ladd, but at least the Church of that period did overcome paganism; 'how far are we getting with our easy-going ideas about baptism and church membership?'

Ladd's ideas about the Eucharist and baptism, as well as on the calendar and lectionary reform, anticipated in the 1930s what would emerge in the next generation as major accomplishments of the Liturgical Movement. The calendar of saints' days should be revised to include examples of holiness relevant to modern people, Ladd said, the redundant season of pre-Lent eliminated, and the joyful nature of the 'great fifty days of Eastertide' emphasized by having the people stand for the preface of the eucharistic prayer. There should be a revised eucharistic lectionary, drawn up 'with the help of modern Biblical scholarship', to allow for an Old Testament lesson and a better selection of other Scripture. Even a little spontaneity of prayer in the Eucharist might not be a bad thing, he suggested.

Ladd created a setting at Berkeley Divinity School that attracted disciples and exposed leaders of parish worship to the liturgical principles exemplified in *Prayer Book Interleaves*. A line of influence descends from Ladd to one of his foremost liturgical disciples, Massey H. Shepherd, Jr. (1913–90), an architect of the 1979 Prayer Book, and thence to Associated Parishes, the organization Shepherd helped found in 1946 which drew into its orbit and formed the outlook of most of the people responsible for producing the 1979 Book of Common Prayer. In a sense, Ladd is on every page of the Prayer Book today. The 1979 book recognized that fundamental sociological changes had altered the relation of the

Church to its surrounding world. It explicitly provided for the liturgical priesthood of the laity, recognized the Eucharist as 'the principal act of Christian worship on the Lord's Day', and articulated the social consequences of Eucharist and baptism for a Church no longer coterminous with society, which must be intentional in making disciples. With that book, Ladd's cause was taken up by the whole Church.

SELECT BIBLIOGRAPHY

M. Moriarty, *The Liturgical Revolution: Prayer Book Revision and Associated Parishes: A Generation of Change in the Episcopal Church*, Church Hymnal, 1996.

M. Moriarty, 'William Palmer Ladd and the Origins of the Episcopal Liturgical Movement', *Church History* 64 (September 1995), pp. 438–51.

Prayer Book Interleaves: Some Reflections on How the Book of Common Prayer Might Be Made More Influential in Our English-Speaking World, Oxford University Press, 1942; 2nd edn, Seabury Press, 1957.

9

A. G. HEBERT

CHRISTOPHER IRVINE

Gabriel Hebert (1886–1963), the son of a clergyman of some private means, trod what was a familiar Anglican path: public school, Oxbridge, and ordination. He was educated at Harrow, an undergraduate at New College, Oxford, and a year at Cuddesdon before ordination. While serving a curacy in the Yorkshire town of Horbury he received an invitation to join Herbert Kelly, the theological maverick and quixotic founder of the Society of the Sacred Mission, in setting up a theological college in Japan. He had been deeply irritated and irresistibly attracted by Kelly's writings, and had first been introduced to the Society of the Sacred Mission by David Jenks. As an undergraduate Hebert had gained a First in Greats and a First in Theology, but his health was not robust. He was temperamentally diffident and physically awkward. He joined the teaching staff at Kelham, but never joined Kelly in Japan. He did not prove to be a good lecturer, and in 1920 was sent to work as a missionary priest in South Africa, where he was professed as a brother of the Society of the Sacred Mission.

In South Africa Hebert fulfilled a number of different and demanding roles, which included some elementary theological teaching at Modderport. He worked with others on the Sesotho translation of the Prayer Book, and in 1921 drafted a series of initiation rites as a contribution to the expected revision of services by the Church of the Province of South Africa. Although these rites drew heavily from the structure and vocabulary of the Book of Common Prayer and the pre-Reformation Sarum rite, they reflected the needs of the missionary situation in which adult initiation was normative practice, and the two forms of baptism fulfilled the pastoral need for liturgical rites to be designed to address those for whom they are intended. So these draft rites included a form for the admission to preparation for baptism, which was intended for use during the main Sunday celebration; and separate orders for the baptism of adults and the baptism of infants. Both these rites included the giving of the white robe and a lighted candle as post-baptismal ceremonies. The draft form for confirmation included the account of the apostles Peter and John being sent to the newly baptized in Samaria, from the Acts of the Apostles, a reading which was supposed to give apostolic warrant for the practice of confirmation, and directed that the bishop anoint each candidate with the oil of chrism. This liturgical project shows Hebert's informed interest in liturgiology, but it is not in liturgy, in any specialized academic sense, that we find his greatest contribution to the worshipping life of the Church. His interests were wide ranging, and his most significant contribution to Christian thought and worship was his influence on the movement of liturgical renewal, a contribution which was driven and informed by his extensive work as an ecumenist and a biblical scholar.

In 1925 Hebert came to England on furlough, but he was never to return to South Africa. He resumed teaching, and with others at Kelham became involved in the work of the Student Christian Movement, a significant cradle of ecumenism. He had caught Fr Kelly's vision of the catholicity of the Church, but the combination of his child-like enthusiasm and doctrinal conservatism often resulted in attitudes which some observers reasonably considered to be inconsistent. In 1928 he was sent on a visit to Sweden and Denmark. He was an astute observer of the liturgical practice of the Swedish and Danish Churches, but more significantly, he discovered the work of Yngve Brilioth, the son-in-law of that great prophet of Christian unity and Archbishop of Uppsala, Nathan Söderblom (1866–1931). As a young historian Brilioth had researched the Oxford Movement and its effect of raising the sacramental consciousness of the Church of England. But what caught Hebert's attention was his work on the Eucharist, *Nattvarden i evangeliskt gudstjänstliv*. This book penetrated eighteenth and nineteenth-century Swedish pietism and sought to recover the eucharistic and liturgical teaching of Reformers Luther, Calvin and Zwingli, and offered an ecumenically sensitive comparative analysis of Anglican, Reformed, Scottish and Swedish eucharistic rites, arranged under five headings: thanksgiving, communion, commemoration, sacrifice and presence. Much of the detailed scholarship in this work has been superseded, and the omission of eschatology as a heading particularly strikes the contemporary reader. But in his day, Hebert clearly regarded Brilioth's study of the Eucharist as an important source for liturgical renewal and as an impetus towards making the celebration of the Eucharist central to the worshipping life of the Church. Hebert, a gifted linguist, translated a shortened text of Brilioth's eucharistic study, and it was published with the English title *Eucharistic Faith and Practice: Catholic and Evangelical*. Later, Hebert was to introduce to English theologians the work of Gustav Aulén and Anders Nygren. Hebert had a gift for friendship, and throughout his life valued his Scandinavian connections. His advice was sought by the Swedish Church Renewal Movement, and he offered both encouragement and criticism, warning against ritualism and narrow Catholic partisanship

Hebert's ecumenical involvement increased, both in England, on the Continent, and latterly in Australia, where he was a prime mover in establishing the Week of Prayer for Christian Unity. He wrote extensively on matters of ecclesiology, and although he stuck rigidly to the traditional threefold ministry of deacons, priests and bishops, as a historically given structure of the visible Church, he came to soften his arguments and began to suggest that it was not necessary to adhere rigidly to any particular theory of apostolic succession. The extent of Hebert's influence was considerable. The Congregationalist scholar Horton Davies, the author of the five-volume work *Worship and Theology in England*, claimed that Hebert's greatest achievement was helping people through his writing, teaching and personal example to appreciate the centrality of worship to the life of the Church. Hebert repeatedly argued that the

Church was most clearly seen to be the Church when the people of God gathered for worship. He contributed a lucidly written anatomy of worship from an Anglican perspective in *Ways of Worship*. Hebert's influence on Leslie Brown was also significant. Leslie Brown was an Anglican Evangelical priest who played a key role in drawing up the liturgy for the Church of South India, where, as Colin Buchanan has commented, the process of liturgical revision, which has preoccupied the Church during the second half of the twentieth century, all began. Brown recorded how he had been 'indoctrinated' by Hebert's *Liturgy and Society* (1935) and *The Parish Communion* (1937). Undoubtedly these two volumes represent Hebert's impact upon liturgical renewal.

Liturgy and Society shows Hebert as a man of his times. It reflects a masculine world, and in part strikes the reader as being quaint. But it also shows Hebert as a man of his times in a more positive sense. He emerges as a person who was aware of the contemporary shifts in the currents of thought, and who was critical of many unquestioned cultural and social assumptions. In the book he drew from, and introduced his readers to, a number of significant and previously unheard voices. There were the insights of Swedish theologians, and frequent references to the *mysterientheologie* of Ildefons Herwegen, the abbot of the Rhineland Abbey of Maria Laach, which had become the centre of the Continental Liturgical Movement. More predictably, Hebert was indebted to the thought of F. D. Maurice (Fr Kelly's source of theological inspiration) and, interestingly, cited the work of the poet and critic T. S. Eliot, and the controversial novelist D. H. Lawrence. In this book Hebert challenged his readers to abandon liberalism. He did not suggest a retreat to some imagined and idealized Christian past, but a move forward in the creation of Christian society. In his view the most invidious effect of liberalism was individualism, which Hebert saw as the greatest impediment to worship. Hebert insisted that worship was central to the whole Christian endeavour. Christianity could not be a privatized religion, or an individual life choice, because it was essentially the means of entering into and participating in a common life.

Worship, he argued, was essentially corporate and was the primary expression of Christian belief. Furthermore, through their participation in the Church's prayer, Christians realized their identity as the Body of Christ, and were challenged to exercise their ministry in the making of a more humane world. The Eucharist was the centre point, the centre of worship, and the means whereby worshippers were sustained in their corporate identity of being the Body of Christ, and enlivened as the People of God. The Eucharist was the point of meeting with the triune God. As such a privileged occasion, it was a point of transformation and the re-making of that new humanity which is shown in Christ. Inspired by a rather romantic view of liturgical history, Hebert seized upon the offertory as being a key and pivotal point in the divine commerce with the world, which he believed was transacted through the eucharistic action. In characteristic vein he once opined that the bread and wine brought to the altar at the offertory is

> drawn from the world of nature as that is exploited by manufacture and commerce. In the act of consecration judgement is passed upon the world in which bread and wine are cornered by speculators and adulterated by manufacturers; a world in which the interests of money actually misrepresent God's bounty and create poverty. The holy Eucharist takes the common means of bodily sustenance for which the sinful world struggles and swindles and restores them to their proper place as the instruments of human fellowship.

The Eucharist was not only the point of transformation, where human society found its cohesion in Christ, but also the point from which worshippers were sent out to exercise their ministry in the circumstances of their daily lives. Once again, this conviction was learnt from Maria Laach, and has informed subsequent drafting of postcommunion prayers and concluding dismissals in revised rites, with their accent on 'service' and the 'sending out' of worshippers to take their part in the liturgy of the world, through the practical outworking of the Christian vision in society. Further theoretical and practical considerations regarding the programme for the renewal of worship were offered in the essays contained in Hebert's symposium *The Parish Communion* (1937), which was arguably the greatest influence on the worshipping life of the Church of England during the middle decades of the twentieth century. The book met a real need, and some 2,500 copies were sold in the first nine months. The contributors included the theologian Austin Farrer, Gregory Dix, and Henry de Candole, who was later to be a key leader in the Parish and People Movement. In setting out the case for the centrality of the Eucharist, Hebert was driven not so much by a desire to change the pattern of Anglican Sunday worship in the parish, but by an ecclesiology dominated by the model of the Body of Christ, which required the celebration of the Eucharist as its primary liturgical expression.

Hebert accentuated the corporate nature of worship and insisted that liturgy was primarily *action*, something that was done by clergy and people together. The point was taken up and substantiated, albeit with some special pleading, by Gregory Dix in *The Shape of the Liturgy* (1945). Recovering this sense of liturgy as action helped Hebert to see that participation in worship was the most formative experience in the life of a Christian, and one which could have a greater impact on people than any mode of teaching. This, of course, is a crucial insight for the pastoral liturgist.

Finally, Hebert's name is also associated with the kind of biblical theology which became prevalent in the 1940s and 1950s. His work in this field, particularly his concern to relate the New Testament and the Hebrew Bible, have now been largely superseded by the work of canon and literary critics. But his work on the psalms, and identification of the worshipping traditions of the Church as providing a significant context for the reading of the Bible as Scripture, suggest a kind of liturgical hermeneutic which is of interest to the liturgical theologian, and could well provide some principles to help guide the liturgist in the task of lectionary revision.

SELECT BIBLIOGRAPHY

The Authority of the Old Testament, Faber & Faber, 1947.
(Translator) Y. Brilioth, *Eucharistic Faith and Practice: Catholic and Evangelical*, SPCK, 1930.
The Form of the Church, Faber & Faber, 1944, revised edn, 1954.
God's Kingdom and Ours, SCM Press, 1959.
Liturgy and Society, Faber & Faber, 1935.
Ways of Worship, SCM Press, 1951.
When Israel Came out of Egypt, SCM Press, 1961.

A comprehensive list of Hebert's published work is given in C. Irvine, *Worship, Church and Society*, Canterbury Press, 1993.

10

PERCY DEARMER

DONALD GRAY

In the Church of England there are two extremes of opinion about the content and conduct of public worship: one which is ready to treat it with cavalier abandon with little regard for its structures, and another which can be characterized as being pernickety and fussy, concerned with details, rubrics and suchlike. In between, in the realms of the always reliable Anglican *vedia media*, there is the opportunity to mock and caricature either of these polarized positions.

For many years it was thought smart to pour scorn on the work of Percy Dearmer, particularly on his first (and most important) publication *The Parson's Handbook*. Certainly it could be represented as the work of an *enfant terrible*. On its publication, in the spring of 1899, Dearmer had only been ordained seven years, was still an assistant priest – and that at a proprietary chapel.

These were the days of widespread liturgical anarchy in the Church of England. The ritualists were abroad in the land. The High Church, Oxford, Tractarian movement had by this time divided on liturgical matters. One section now looked unashamedly to the Roman Catholic Church for its rules and regulations, following, usually uncritically, the prevailing customs of the Western Church. It was said that the rituals, and ecclesiastical millinery, of the churches within this tradition were more often determined by where on the Continent the parish priest had spent his last holiday than anything else. They were anxious to rid the Church of England, as speedily as possible, of Protestant error. The result was 'often bogus Baroque and Rococo', wrote Peter Anson.

Whereas there were those who tried to be what later came to be known as 'Prayer Book Catholics'. There had been the work of the Cambridge Camden Society in the 1840s, but it was now largely forgotten, or thought to be hopelessly out of date. It was Dearmer, the Alcuin Club (which published some of his early writing) and the Wareham Guild (which he founded in 1912) that provided a scholarly basis for those who wished to adopt a more Anglican approach to worship. They needed guidance about the way in which they could affirm the catholicity of the Church of England and also its continuity with, and within, the worship of the undivided Church. Such clergy and laity required help in identifying the ceremonies and rituals which would assist this affirmation without jettisoning the underlying principles of the Reformation settlement of the Church.

Dearmer's book found a ready and receptive public. First published in March 1899, it had been reprinted by July and then again in November. It was not, of course, without its critics, so Dearmer needed to add an extra preface on reprinting. In this he explained that the *Handbook* was not intended for the extreme, 'still less is it meant to hound any parson on to extravagances, or to provide a "ritualistic" manifesto'. He asserted that it was, like the Church of England, comprehensive. Some may dislike the chasuble, and some the black gown; for both, Dearmer says, provision is made in his book.

> If I had written a Cricketer's Handbook, no one would have complained of *minutiae*; if a Cookery Book, every one would have been up in arms against me for the superficial treatment of a great and serious subject. Yet I cannot help thinking that the worship of God calls for as careful treatment as the playing of games, and that an orderly complement of accessories is as necessary in the church as in the scullery.

James Adderley, the Priest-in-Charge of the Berkeley Chapel, Mayfair, for whom Dearmer was working at the time, claimed to have invented the phrase 'British Museum religion'. This was the jibe by which the *Handbook*'s detractors (down the years) used to pour scorn on its principles. It was true, the book was the result of much research and long hours in the Reading Room of the British Museum, but Adderley also confidently asserted that Dearmer was 'just the man to rescue liturgiology from the pedantry of the mere man of letters and make it attractive to the whole church'. However, it must not be thought that the *Handbook* ignored the researches of other contemporary scholars. Already in 1899 Dearmer was expressing his obligation to F. E. Brightman and W. H. Frere 'for their suggestions and amendments'. He was not working in isolation. Dearmer believed that although the early Tractarians had often been men of learning and had revived liturgical scholarship, setting themselves to recover what the Puritans had lost, none the less in some areas they were not sufficiently equipped to do the task properly. Again, although leaders of the Gothic revival, they were responsible for some of its worst features. To them, as far as the adornments of churches went, everything seemed right if only it was clothed in imitation Gothic detail.

In 1900 Dearmer was given the opportunity to work out his ideas practically, pastorally and parochially – he was appointed Vicar of St Mary's, Primrose Hill. That north London church quickly became a mecca for those who recognized the value of Dearmer's principles. He did not disappoint them. One of his earliest actions was to whitewash the red brick walls of the church; this was followed by lowering the reredos, lengthening the altar, removing the tabernacle, reducing the number of candles and, finally, adding a dorsal and side curtains at the altar. It was now a complete *Parson's Handbook* eastend, around which the Eucharist was celebrated in the style and manner the book had advocated.

If St Mary's became a model for visual aesthetic standards, it also became a beacon in the gloom which had begun to envelop the music of the Church. After some initial reluctance, mainly among High Churchmen, hymnody had now assumed major importance in Anglican worship. The days of the parish band were long since gone, and it had been replaced in the chancel, rather than a gallery, by a surpliced choir (gradually surpliced, despite the perseverance of lingering Low-Church protests). The hymn book used was usually *Hymns Ancient and Modern*, itself a product of the cautious High-Church school. The book had accumulated to itself, over its many editions, a vast repertoire of hymns and tunes, many of which would not easily survive the fierce light of informed poetical or musical examination. The need to provide a hymn book which was more worthy of its task had already been recognized, but it required the enthusiasm and dynamism of a Dearmer to bring together men of calibre who could, and would, revolutionize the standard of hymnody in England.

The task additionally involved making available other traditional liturgical texts in English, with appropriate music, in order that they might be accessible and useable at the parish level. This was the great achievement of *The English Hymnal* – the eventual product of this work.

Dearmer attracted to his aid such writers as Laurence Housman and Robert Bridges. Together they tackled the work of providing for the first time in Church of England worship such hymns as Bunyan's 'He who would valiant be'; the work of J. G. Whittier ('Immortal love', 'Dear Lord and Father'); Christina Rossetti's 'In the bleak mid-winter'; F. K. Chesterton's 'O God of earth and altar'. Next they needed to recruit a musical editor, and both Cecil Sharp and Henry Scott Holland recommended the same name, a rising composer and the son of the former Rector of Down Ampney, Gloucestershire – Ralph Vaughan Williams. Through Vaughan Williams's influence via *The English Hymnal* and later *Songs of Praise* (in which Dearmer was also involved), the standard of hymnody and its performance rose considerably.

The English Hymnal was published on Ascension Day 1906, but *Songs of Praise* did not appear until 1925. By then Dearmer had been visited by the vicissitudes of life both personally and ecclesiastically. The 1914–18 War provided tragedy in different ways. A lifelong Christian Socialist who had been inspired at Oxford by Charles Gore and was Secretary of the University branch of Stewart Headlam's Guild of St Matthew, he found the outbreak of war between 'the brotherhood of man' difficult and painful. He took leave of absence from Primrose Hill to work with his wife Mabel in the nursing units in Serbia. Mabel died of typhus at Kragujevatz, and three months later he heard of the death of his son Christopher at Suvla Bay.

Dearmer resigned his living and worked for a while in France for the YMCA before, having married again, going on a prolonged tour of India and the United States. On returning to England, rather than taking another parochial charge he accepted the offer of the chair of Ecclesiastical Art at King's College, London. Then followed twelve years of varying activity. Besides his work at King's there was an inter-denominational experiment at the Guildhouse, Holy Trinity Sloane Square and, all the while, a good deal of writing. It was during this period that he developed what was at the time an unfashionable interest in the ministry of women, encouraging the witness of Maude Royden. Additionally he continued his involvement in the ministry of healing, which dated back to his part in the foundation of the Guild of Health in 1904.

He wrote on *The Art of Public Worship*, and on *Art and Religion*, compiled a *Short Handbook of Public Worship* and a popular *Story of the Prayer Book*. One of the books he wrote at that time made a significant contribution to the movement for the encouragement of the Parish Communion. It was entitled *The Truth about Fasting*. In many High Church parishes the establishment of a mid-morning service with general communion was proving difficult because of the application of the rule concerning the fast before communion. Dearmer's book questioned some of the assumptions behind this custom, and attempted to persuade his readers towards a more relaxed attitude.

After these twelve somewhat 'wilderness years' it was perhaps not surprising that it should be a Labour Prime Minister, Ramsey MacDonald, who came to the rescue. Recognizing that Dearmer's talents were being wasted, the Prime Minister offered to nominate him to the Crown as a Canon of Westminster, and Dearmer accepted. Sadly he only had five years at the Abbey, but during that time he was able to build on an old friendship with the Sacrist, the formidable Jocelyn Perkins, a fellow advocate of the English Use.

Dearmer was a unique combination of a liturgical scholar deeply influenced by his Christian Socialism, who believed that the Eucharist is an extension of the Incarnation; and an aesthete who believed that art, and not least those aspects of art we employ in the liturgy, opens to us one of the doors into the Kingdom of Heaven. Dearmer was convinced that art is the one language common to all mankind, and the *lingua franca* of heaven as well as earth. For him the study of liturgy was undertaken in order that we might 'best serve God for his own sake'. Good liturgy may not be a panacea for filling churches, but he was confident that worship done well, in beautiful surroundings, with good music, can be evangelistic, and therefore it is our solemn duty to take the greatest possible care over everything we do in church.

SELECT BIBLIOGRAPHY

Art and Religion, SCM Press, 1925.
The Art of Public Worship, Mowbray, 1919.
Fifty Pictures of Gothic Altars, Alcuin Club Collections X, 1910.
The Ornaments of the Minister, Mowbray, 1908; new edn, 1920.
The Parson's Handbook, 1st edn, Grant Richards, 1899; 12th edn, Oxford University Press, 1932.
A Short Handbook of Public Worship. The Story of the Prayer Book, Oxford University Press, 1931.
The Story of the Prayer Book, Oxford University Press, 1933.
The Truth about Fasting, Rivington, 1928.

11

R. D. RICHARDSON

MARTIN DUDLEY

Hans Lietzmann's *Mass and Lord's Supper* first appeared in German in 1926. Lietzmann (1875–1942) was a distinguished New Testament scholar and ecclesiastical historian, a classicist and a palaeographer, and he had a strong interest in the scientific study of the liturgy. His edition of the Gregorian Sacramentary (from a manuscript at Aachen) was for a long time the only scholarly one. *Messe und Herrenmahl*, published by Walter de Gruyter in Berlin, was subtitled *Eine Studie zur Geschichte der Liturgie*. The German text ran to some 263 pages but the English translation, by Dorothea Reeves, published by Brill of Leiden, runs to nearly 800 pages. Only 215 of them are Lietzmann; the remainder a 'Further Inquiry' by R. D. Richardson (1893–1989). Begun in 1953, the 'Further Inquiry' reached its conclusion – much to the publisher's relief – in 1978.

R. D. Richardson was born in 1893 and studied theology with distinction at Hertford College, Oxford, graduating in 1921. He added an Oxford BLitt in 1923 (and the BD and DD in 1952) and was ordained deacon in 1923, being prepared at Ripon Hall, the liberal theological college now amalgamated with Cuddesdon. After serving his title in Worcester diocese, Richardson moved to Birmingham, where he served for twenty-one years, thirteen as Vicar of Harborne, 1934–47. He was Select Preacher at the University of Cambridge in 1934, and Examining Chaplain to Bishop Barnes of Birmingham, 1936–52. In 1947 he succeeded H. D. A. Major, founder of *The Modern Churchman*, as Principal of Ripon College. After five years he returned to parish ministry as Rector of Boyton with Sherrington in Wiltshire, where he retired and lived until he died, on 30 March 1989.

It was at Harborne that his interest in liturgy developed, combining the scholarly with the practical as he produced his own alternative order of Holy Communion. The episcopate of E. W. Barnes, one of the most prominent Modern Churchmen, involved considerable conflict with Birmingham's Anglo-Catholics. Richardson, though a modernist, counted himself as a Catholic with a high view of the sacraments, but he was opposed, as his bishop was, to the Romanizing tendency of so many of the city's clergy. To counter their interpolated rites, Richardson produced his own 'Harborne Rite', intended as 'an eirenicon to all parties in the Church of England, since official Prayer Book revision has so far failed to win agreement'. It combined material from 1662 and 1928 with material drawn from ancient liturgies, and included, well ahead of its time, alternative confessions of faith. The Rite was intended to be 'another Alternative Use' that might influence future liturgical development, and it attracted attention and criticism. *The Church Times* attacked it in 1938, when Dean Inge was among those who defended it, and in 1940 when Richardson defended himself. In 1942 Richardson wrote to Archbishop Temple, in response to a pronouncement on liturgical illegalities, defending himself:

> [B]ut I trust Your Grace will believe that my use of [the Harborne Rite] is governed by no irresponsible or unconsidered mood. The neglect of the Report of the Royal Commission on Ecclesiastical Discipline (1906) has been accompanied by such an extension of the illegalities there condemned, and by such a tendency to regard them as permissible now that they have the authority of long precedent, that I feel that Catholic-minded churchmen of the Liberal school must win a like authority for the changes which seem to them required by their devotional needs. But I have always said . . . that if others would cease to vary the 1662 Rite I would do the same; and I believe

> that my action has done something to restore at least a desire for order in the Church of England.

Temple replied, and his letter tells us a good deal about what occupied the archiepiscopal mind two weeks after the battle of El Alamein:

> I do myself regard all unauthorised experiments with the Holy communion Service as really undesirable because that service is so emphatically the service of the whole Church. Of course I recognise that one school of thought in the Church has taken the view that the Use of Western Christendom generally supplied them with a certain measure of authority for the variations which they introduce, and I very deeply deplore this fact. I could not undertake to offer any direct criticism of the form that you yourself occasionally use, but of course it does depart further from anything that has been traditional than most others. I will not say more than that. I expect you feel yourself to be responsible for maintaining a certain standpoint, and therefore almost obliged to maintain the use of this rite unless all other deviations from the prayer book in other quarters are abandoned. On that position also I make no comment, but should like you to know that I recognise how a man may be led to adopt it, and to maintain it.

The Harborne Rite was very advanced for its time, and some of the issues it raised are only now being addressed in the new round of liturgical revision.

In 1943 Richardson set out his views on worship to the conference of Modern Churchmen. He was opposed to the 'theological supernaturalism' which had been imposed upon the gospel and to any 'interventionary view of God'. This provided him with a liturgical agenda:

> Religion, indeed, calls for more poetry, and for less evident theology, as its vehicle of worship and praise. This means a new creed, written in the spirit of *Te Deum*. It means the removal from worship of the more technical

> theological terms, like grace, salvation and redemption. It means a thorough recasting of the Psalter. It means a very careful choice of Bible readings, directed towards teaching the right method of divine governance and guidance in creation, in history and in the human soul; and the truth in myth and allegory must be plain for all to see. It means bringing the figure of Jesus into the forefront of worship; focusing attention on His gospel, and laying emphasis on Christian discipleship as the way to reasonable, brave, unselfish, happy service of God. The hesitating English instinct towards liturgical reform must be hastened, in a genuinely religious and creative spirit.

The Eucharist needed particular revision to make it

> more consistent with its central theme; that of personal consecration to God through the Christ Who, under the forms of bread and wine, communicates to us His own Self. Through communion with him, we ourselves become full persons, with breadth of interest and fullness of energy devoted to spiritual ends; capable of uniting and constituting a Christian society.

Richardson believed that the most effective way to promote community through public worship was by removing all that makes it exclusive, what he called the 'ministerial, credal and sacramental barriers'. He was, therefore, vigorously opposed to the sacerdotal and dogmatic aspects of Anglo-Catholicism, and this opposition was expressed through liturgical practice. The Mass he saw as entirely controlled by the 'myth and ritual pattern'. The figure of Jesus within this pattern of Sacrifice and Atonement had become Victim and Mediator. Communion was 'a participation in a supernatural life dispersed sacramentally from the altar – according to the "sacrifice and burnt-offering" view of the relation of man to God.' He embraced the view of communion as a fellowship meal centred on Christ.

In 1950, and now a leading Modernist figure, he again set out the requirements for worship. His thinking was informed by the writings of T. H. Gaster and E. O. James on myth and ritual. Christian rites – coronations, ordinations, initiation, Mass, marriage, last rites, processions and mystery plays, seasonal games and burlesques – emerged from and were set into a mythical pre-scientific world. With new knowledge the Reformers had gone some way towards rescuing religious practice from superstition, giving humanity a new dignity and making the person and character of Jesus himself central to worship. The Prayer Book specifically repudiated 'things which are untrue, uncertain and superstitious', 'stories and legends', and 'a multitude of ceremonies' that 'did more confound and darken, than declare and set forth, Christ's benefits'. Anglo-Catholicism and the Romanizing tendency seemed determined to undo this significant Reformation work. Ancient patterns revealed the deepest human needs, which found expression in worship, and these needs revealed human beings as spiritual, moral and rational. The needs, not least that of dealing with the mystery of evil, remained today, but in a new, enlightened, scientific and non-supernatural context. Richardson wanted to liberate Christ and the gospel from the mythological perspective and set him against the background of the universe as disclosed by science.

> In the worship of the new Reformation, then, all the deepest needs of our spiritual nature will be expressed and fully met. And the Services will converge upon, and lead the worshipper directly to, God as He is most intimately Self-revealed in that Perfect Life which once was lived in Galilee. When our forms of Service have achieved this, they will also be a perfect means of communion whereby the power of Christ's endless life in God will be quickened within us and among us.

Richardson was, however, a scholar unable to reject or ignore his source material, and he needed to find a clear basis in the tradition for his rejection of mythical interpretations. He was drawn to Lietzmann's analysis of the dual origins of the eucharistic rite, and so began his prolonged inquiry. So prolonged was it that it fell behind the process of liturgical revision, in which Richardson took no part, but the intention of the inquiry remained the same throughout, though not made explicit; it was that of justifying the Harborne Rite in its rejection of supernaturalism and in its acceptance of biblical-critical perspectives on eucharistic origins. He knew at the end what an adequate rite would be. It was much as he had conceived it at the beginning.

> It will set forth liturgically and dramatically an interpretation of the events in the Upper Room as summing up the whole meaning of Jesus' life and death; in other words it will not be without a theology and a ritual pattern. But the historical figure must control all developments, and neither fade in, nor be metamorphosed by, the dramatic-dogmatic forms. By these, the worshipper should be led directly to his Lord . . . The sacerdotal, hieratic, sacrificial conception of the eucharist, which took its rise from the Marcan development and is exemplified most perfectly in the Roman rite, wherein the priest performs an act of universal and even cosmic significance, should recede into the background as the philosophically ultimate meaning of it all. The eucharistic rite of the Book of Common Prayer represents a step in the direction we have indicated, but the Church of England needs to implement more fully the character and constitution that it adopted at the Reformation.

SELECT BIBLIOGRAPHY

An Alternative Order of Holy Communion, James Clarke & Co, 1940.

'Berakah and Eucharistia', *Church Quarterly Review* (the offprint has no date).

Causes of the Present Conflict of Ideals in the Church of England, Murray, 1923.

Christian Belief and Practice, James Clarke & Co, 1941.

'Christian Worship in the New Reformation', a paper read before the Modern Churchmen's Conference, August 1950.

'The Doctrinal Characteristics of the Church of England', *Modern Churchman*, 1935.

'The Doctrine of the Trinity; its development, difficulties and value', *Harvard Theological Review* vol. 36, no. 2 (April 1943).
'Eastern and Western Liturgies: The Primitive Basis of their Later Differences', *Harvard Theological Review* vol. 42, no. 2 (April 1949).
'Further Inquiry' in Hans Lietzmann, *Mass and the Lord's Supper*, Brill, 1978.
The Gospel of Modernism, 1st edn, Skeffington, 1933; 2nd edn, 1935.
'Jesus and Christian Institutions', *Modern Churchman Conference Number*, September 1946.
'The Lord's Prayer as an Early Eucharistia', *Anglican Theological Review*, April 1957.
'Modernism', *The Free Catholic* vol. 12, no. 7 (July 1927).
'The Mystics and the Sacraments', a paper read before the Modern Churchmen's Conference, September 1926.
'The National Church and Divine Worship', *Modern Churchman Conference Number*, September 1943.
'The Place of Luke in the Eucharistic Tradition', K. Aland, F. L. Cross, J. Danielou et al. (eds), *Studia Evangelica*, Berlin, 1959, pp. 665–75.
'Psalms as Christian Prayers and Praises', *Anglican Theological Review* vol. 42, no. 4 (Oct. 1960).
The Psalms as Christian Prayers and Praises, privately printed, n.d.

12

E. C. RATCLIFF

CHRISTOPHER IRVINE

A bibliography of E. C. Ratcliff's published works was published to mark the seventy-fifth anniversary of the Alcuin Club, and although it records that Ratcliff (1896–1967) wrote no major books, it shows that he was a prodigious writer of articles and reviews. These reflect the necessarily broad range of interests of a university teacher and his engagement with ongoing scholarly research. Ratcliff's elegantly crafted reviews and essays revealed the careful work of a scholar, but his articles in the Chichester diocesan *Gazette* were often rather pointed contributions to current liturgical debate. With acerbic wit Ratcliff once exclaimed that his subject was liturgy and not circus, indicating that it was the disciplined and detailed examination of texts, linguistic competence and historical criticism which were the proper tools and occupations of the liturgist. This was not, however, to say that he viewed the liturgist's task as a narrow specialism, or simply an archaeological exercise. On one occasion he opined that liturgical work required a deep understanding both of the notions underlying any liturgical form, and a recognition of the diversity of liturgical traditions in which these forms expressed themselves. Contexts as well as texts, in other words, needed to be understood.

In a friendly review of the Ordinal of the Church of South India he noted that 'to compose a rite is easy enough; but to compose one well is the reverse of easy'. This comment reveals something of Ratcliff's wry humour and sense of irony, but typically this humour was concealed by the mannered style of an essentially private man. His pupils often found him to be kind and his colleagues respected his learning. He was reticent in company and was considered to be an enigma. Even his friend Arthur Couratin admitted that no one really knew him well, although his devotion to his cats was legendary.

Ratcliff was the only son of a comfortable and cultured family and was educated at Merchant Taylor's School, where he excelled at classics. He gained a scholarship at St John's College, Cambridge, but his entry was deferred because of the outbreak of the First World War. Deemed unfit for military service he elected to work for the YMCA in India, from 1916 to 1918. This was to bring him into contact with Syrian Christians in Malabar, and stimulate a lifelong interest. A breakdown in health resulted in an early return from India to England. Later, in mid-career, Ratcliff had to take two years out of academic life for rest and recuperation, and his uncertain health became an increasing anxiety in his latter years.

The Indian experience was undoubtedly formative for his subsequent work as a liturgist. His first scholarly article, 'The Original Form of the Anaphora of Addai and Mari', sought to uncover the antecedents of the liturgy of the Malabar Church in India, and it was this work which secured his reputation as a meticulous scholar of the Syrian liturgical tradition. In 1963 he published an article on the liturgical homilies of Narsai (a fifth-century East Syrian theological poet associated with Edessa), and two years later Ratcliff published his work on the Syrian baptismal tradition. In this suggestive work, Ratcliff described how this tradition came to be assimilated and embellished in fourth-century Jerusalem.

Ratcliff's first liturgical project, written in conjunction with J. C. Winslow, the examining chaplain to the Bishop of Bombay, was published while he was still an undergraduate at St John's College, Cambridge. Winslow recognized in Ratcliff a flair for liturgy, the gifts of a linguist, and a sensitivity to the Indian religious consciousness, and sought his help in setting out the case for the need of a eucharistic liturgy for the Indian church. The resulting volume, *The Eucharist in India,* consisted of three substantial essays and a eucharistic rite, which was presented as a model of the kind of liturgy which would be appropriate for use within an Indian cultural setting. In the first essay, Winslow set out the reasons why a new liturgy was required for the different cultural setting of India. The point was reinforced by Ratcliff, who argued that a revision of the 1662 Communion Office would not be suitable for an Indian setting, not least because the theological controversies of Reformation Europe, which had influenced its form and content, were not an intrinsic part of Christian history in India. Ratcliff's proposal was to uncover an earlier history and dig deeper to the roots of Christian life in India, and these he believed were to be located in East Syria and the ancient liturgy of Jerusalem. The model rite contained in *The Eucharist in India* was basically a shortened form of the Syrian version of the Liturgy of St James, which in its original form was the local liturgy of Jerusalem, but soon came to be adopted and developed in Antioch. In 1665 the Liturgy of James had been transplanted on to Indian soil, in Malabar, where the majority of the former Nestorian Christians of St Thomas (who until that time had used the East Syrian liturgy of Addai and Mari) had declined the invitation to become a Uniate Church and instead opted to be in communion with the Jacobite Patriarch of Antioch. In proposing an adapted form of the Liturgy of James, regarded by Ratcliff as being unequalled in order and beauty, he and his co-essayists believed that they were opening the doors for the adoption of an authentic inculturated liturgy. (A note in an appendix recommended the use of the chapati rather than wafer bread for communion.) For the young Ratcliff this interest in the forms of prayer from the east opened up a treasure store of Christian spirituality and was more than an academic exercise. Shortly after his death it was rumoured that he had been preparing to become a member of the Orthodox Church.

As a young man Ratcliff had experienced the full panoply of Anglo-Catholic worship at St Peter's Church, Streatham, in south London. In later life, and largely through gaining an extensive knowledge of Anglican history, Ratcliff came to feel an unease with the claims of his Anglo-Catholic contemporaries and their forms of worship. He had been ordained in 1922, and after serving a two-year curacy returned to Cambridge to take up the post of Vice-Principal at Westcott House, a step which led him into an academic career rather than an ecclesiastical one. He did not particularly enjoy preaching and as time went on felt increasingly out of place in clerical gatherings. He did, however, have an affection for Ely Cathedral, and his advice on liturgical matters there was sought during his time as a residentiary canon. He took a cautious and conservative line on Prayer Book revision and argued against the inclusion of the epiclesis in the prayer of consecration on the grounds that it was not compatible with the intention and doctrinal framework of the Prayer Book rite. As a scholar, Ratcliff's understanding of the English liturgical tradition and usage was second to none. In 1949 he published a small volume to mark the 400th anniversary of the publication of the first English Prayer Book of Edward Vl, which included some eighty manuscript photographs illustrating its origins and subsequent revisions. In his teaching and writing Ratcliff presented Thomas Cranmer as having been both a cautious scholar and a creative liturgiologist. In Ratcliff's view, Cranmer did not readily dispense with inherited models of liturgical prayer, but equally was never completely circumscribed by them, and argued that his genius was to be seen in the way in which he adapted traditional material to serve his own purposes. Ratcliff believed that the single most important Reformation influence upon Cranmer's thought and work was Luther, a view which has recently been reiterated by the Cambridge English historian Patrick Collinson, who has claimed that Cranmer's 'understanding of the Gospel moved within essentially Lutheran parameters'. Other scholars, of course, might disagree with this assessment. Ratcliff's scholarly engagement with English liturgical history included work on the early Puritan tradition and, more famously, work on that most exotic flower of the English liturgical tradition, the Coronation Service. He was consulted over the service for the Coronation of Queen Elizabeth II, and in 1953 published the service with an extensive historical introduction and a translation of the ceremonial directions of the *Liber Regalis* as an appendix.

Apart from these two slim volumes, Ratcliff's scholarly work is to be found scattered in a number of articles and reviews. His most significant scholarly work has led to further investigations, notably by contemporary scholars such as Bryan Spinks, into the patterns of primitive eucharistic prayers and baptismal practice in the area of the Syrian liturgical tradition. Arguably, Ratcliff's most significant contribution as a scholar was as an Orientalist. His stimulating essay on the 'Original Form of Addai and Mari' is a particular case in point. The anaphora of 'SS Addai and Mari, the blessed apostles' represents a primitive pattern of eucharistic praying which contrasts sharply with the form given in the *Apostolic Tradition*, ascribed to Hippolytus of Rome – a prayer of uncertain status, which was regarded as the earliest fixed form of a eucharistic prayer, and was seized upon during the first fever of liturgical revision in the 1960s as the apogee of eucharistic praying. Although the earliest extant manuscript of *Addai and Mari* is a tenth-century recension, it is thought to contain elements well attested to in the fifth century, and which probably date back to third-century usage in Syria. The present consensus is that the Addai and Mari text, as reconstructed by Gelston and Spinks, reflects the usage of Edessa, the centre of East Syrian Christianity, which for both theological and ideological reasons became increasingly isolated from the wider Christian world, and thereby preserved some of its most ancient and Semitic forms. By this time, however, its influence had moved to Persia and possibly even further east. The liturgical tradition represented by Addai and Mari survived into modern times in the isolated Church of the East, in the Kurdistan mountains, and as already indicated, was the basis of the Malabar liturgy in India.

In his analysis of this anaphora, Ratcliff came to the conclusion that this series of discrete prayers fell somewhere on the continuum between the Christian Agape and the Mass. This conclusion resulted from a rather linear evolutionary model of the development of the eucharistic prayer, a model which fails to take account of the geographical diversity and variety of local liturgical traditions in the early Church. Furthermore, as Ratcliff's conception of a developed eucharistic prayer was constructed from Western sources, principally North Africa and Rome, he had to indulge in some intelligent guesswork to account for what by comparison emerged as the oddities in the Addai and Mari form of eucharistic praying. Elements, such as the epiclesis, for instance, did not fit into his preconceived shape of the structure of a eucharistic prayer, and so it was deemed to be an interpolation. Despite an oblique reference to the institution in the prayer, Ratcliff considered that the absence of a full 'institution narrative' meant that it was defective as a eucharistic prayer. Reflections on the other elements of this prayer were more speculative, and arose from more linguistic considerations. The most famous of these were his observations regarding the *sanctus*. He argued that as there was no direct linking between the individual prayers which preceded and followed the *sanctus*, it was probably a later and intrusive addition to the anaphora. But linguistic considerations alone, of course, are not sufficient to establish such a conclusion. Later, considering the anaphora in the *Apostolic Tradition*, Ratcliff argued that the *sanctus* might originally have come at the end of the eucharistic prayer. This, Ratcliff opined, would have given a fitting climax of praise to the prayer. Apparently, he also came to suggest that this might have been the original place and function of the *sanctus* in the Addai and Mari prayer as well, but in private correspondence with Couratin he admitted that he had been rather obsessive about the subject. Ratcliff's speculative conclusion about the original position of the *sanctus*, which came to be known as the 'climax theory', is unprovable historically, but did strike some liturgical revisers as having some theological rationale and as being devotionally helpful.

The 'climax theory', though historically untenable, is theologically compatible with the notion that the Christian *eucharistia* draws and joins worshippers to the unending praise of heaven, and has commended itself to some modern liturgical revisers. The last three of the six eucharistic prayers included in the English Congregationalist's *Order of Public Worship*, and two of the alternative eucharistic prayers in the Church of England's Liturgical Commission Report *Patterns for Worship* (1989), have the *sanctus* coming at the end of the prayer as a climax of praise.

Ratcliff was a member of the first Church of England

Liturgical Commission in 1955, and served on it until his death in 1967. He commented helpfully on the initial drafts of the proposed Liturgy for Africa, and was also involved in shaping the ordination service, which it was hoped might be adopted after the expected approval of the ill-fated Anglican-Methodist Unity Scheme. He had applauded the Ordinal which had been framed by the Church of South India, with its clear focus on the presiding bishop as both the agent of God and representative of the whole Church, and its culmination in the laying-on of hands and the prayer for the Holy Spirit. Tellingly, he says that such a primitive conception was clearly shown in the ordination rites of the Greek Orthodox and other Eastern Churches, and proffers the view that 'had it not been obscured in the West, and ordination interpreted as a personal act of the bishop conferring certain powers upon the ordinand, not a little controversy, error and division could have been prevented'. On a more domestic front, Ratcliff's expressed views were not always so felicitous, or conciliatory. In 1960 he scuppered the baptismal liturgy which was being experimentally used in the Province of York with savage criticism and caustic wit. The saddest episode came when a joint session of Convocation in April 1967 rejected the phrase 'we offer this bread and this cup' from the eucharistic prayer of the proposed alternative Communion rite. The rejection forced Couratin to resign from the Commission and a few weeks later Ratcliff died. Both the life and work of Edward Ratcliff seem to raise the question of where Anglicans may legitimately find points of theological orientation. As his story unfolds, it appears as though we need not always be looking over our shoulder to Rome.

SELECT BIBLIOGRAPHY

The Coronation Service of Her Majesty Queen Elizabeth II, with a short historical introduction, explanatory notes and an appendix, SPCK and Cambridge University Press, 1953.

'The Eucharistic Office and the Liturgy of St James', J. C. Winslow (ed.), *The Eucharist in India*, Longmans, Green and Company, 1920.

'The Liturgical Work of Archbishop Cranmer', *Journal of Ecclesiastical History* vol. VII, October 1956.

'The Old Syrian Baptismal Tradition and its Resettlement under the Influence of Jerusalem in the Fourth Century', G. J. Cuming, *Studies in Church History* vol. II, Nelson, 1965.

'The Original Form of the Anaphora of Addai and Mari', *Journal of Theological Studies*, vol. XXX, October 1928.

'Puritan Alternatives to the Prayer Book' and 'The Directory and Richard Baxter's Reformed Liturgy', A. M. Ramsey (ed.), *The English Prayer Book 1549–1662*, SPCK, 1963.

'The Sanctus and the Pattern of the Early Anaphora', *Journal of Ecclesiastical History* vol. I, April 1950.

13

HENRY DE CANDOLE

COLIN BUCHANAN

Henry de Candole (1895–1971) contributed strongly to liturgical renewal in the Church of England, without ever being either prominent as a scholar or particularly outstanding on the Liturgical Commission. Instead he contributed both by being at significant places at the right time on the one hand, and by a style of patient advocacy of his principles in a practical way over several decades on the other.

He was born in Bristol of a clerical family in 1895, his father being an Evangelical who in 1902 became vicar of Holy Trinity, Cambridge. Henry, however, came quite early under more 'Catholic' influences, and, when his father returned to Bristol in 1912, the impact of All Saints, Clifton, was apparently decisive. His University life at King's, Cambridge, which followed was split by the Great War, in which time (through ill health) he taught at Marlborough. His brother was killed in the last months of the War, and he became an only son – and his father became a Canon of Westminster, so that Henry, as he returned to Cambridge, had both a base in London and also needy parents who obviously depended much on his spending time with them. Henry was much influenced in this period by Eric Milner White (then Dean of King's) and, as his sense of vocation matured, by B. K. Cunningham, the much-famed principal of Westcott House. He quite soon spent two terms at Westcott preparing for ordination. He was then made deacon by the Bishop of Salisbury on 28 November 1920, and retraced his steps to Marlborough as assistant chaplain.

In 1923 Henry was summoned to Lambeth Palace to become

Domestic Chaplain to Archbishop Randall Davidson, where he remained until 1926. In this capacity he had a vantage point from which he learned much of the Church of England, and in his last few months there he sat in on the first meeting of the House of Bishops to retouch the proposed Prayer Book (i.e. that which was to become the 1927–28 Book). The immediate task was to prepare it for the Church Assembly. This meeting lasted a *fortnight* (a circumstance unimaginable in more recent years). Henry wrote 'I came to realise how entirely ignorant they were about Liturgy, except for a bare fraction – Frere was almost alone . . .' This reflection was not only entirely accurate on any objective view of the personnel concerned, but also affords us an early insight into a mildly critical mind addressing the liturgical field.

Henry did not see this matter through to its debacle, as he had gone off (during the 1926 General Strike) to begin his first parochial ministry, as assistant to an old hero of his, Noel Hudson. Hudson was vicar of St John's, Newcastle, and there Henry had the opportunity to put his 'Catholic' programme into parochial action. A most notable feature of this was a near-insistence on auricular confession (he and Noel Hudson heard about 180 confessions before Easter celebrations in 1927, and all his confirmation candidates did so before first communion). However, whilst through 1927 leaders of Church – and of State – marched and counter-marched and demonstrated about the 'Proposed' Prayer Book, Henry and his High Church vicar were moving towards another of those significant moments that Henry had a gift of being in on. In December 1927, St John's started their '9.15' – the embryonic 'Parish Communion', usually viewed as the pioneer venture from which all subsequent Parish Communions derive. The change (a combination of an 8 o'clock 'early morning communion' and a 10 o'clock 'Children's Eucharist') was based on pastoral considerations – an inclusive service with hymnody and preaching, not so early as to be beyond the likely endeavours of families with young children (or of the newly confirmed), nor so late as to be in danger of breaching the (High Church) rule of fasting. From that time on he became an unswerving advocate of a similar pattern throughout the parishes of the Church of England.

He became (briefly) vicar of St John's, Newcastle, when Noel Hudson was made a bishop in 1931; he went on from there to be chaplain of Peterhouse, Cambridge (1932–34), and of Chichester Theological College (1934–37). He greeted Hebert's *Liturgy and Society* in 1935 as matching his own hopes, and contributed a chapter ('Instruction in Worship') to Hebert's next volume, the symposium *The Parish Communion*, in 1937. It was in 1937 also that he married Frances Cornwall. Then, ever more certain of his Parish Communion ideology and of the need to get it across into parish life, at the same time as getting married he negotiated with Bishop George Bell a uniquely pioneering appointment – that of Chichester Diocesan Liturgical Missioner (which, in the interests of objectivity, one ought to record was the easier for George Bell to approve and inaugurate, as the appointment was unpaid and Henry lived off private means!). In the two years before the Second World War, he conducted in this role regular teaching weeks in several parishes, trying to lay the foundations for changes in parish policy to put the Parish Communion at the centre of parish life. It was a period of his life to which he looked back with great happiness and mild pride.

When the War came, Henry and Frances moved to the country parish of Henfield, where through the War years he gently pursued (and, arguably, in practice vindicated) his policies. Then in 1949 he became suffragan bishop of Knaresborough in the Ripon diocese, and, at almost the same moment, founder-chairman of *Parish and People*. Immediately he had much more public platforms than his country parish had afforded, and he emerged again as the gentle pioneer and thinker of the Parish Communion movement. He wrote pamphlets and contributed articles to journals (including *Parish and People*), and became a foremost popularizer of liturgical renewal. In Ripon diocese he became notable in his practice of confirmations for going to stay in parishes for twenty-four hours prior to the service, and conducting the confirmation (with first communion) within the context of the Parish Communion. He also pioneered in the Church of England (as far as is known) the 'full rite' of adult baptism-confirmation-and-first-communion (interestingly enough, in a conservative evangelical parish – St George's, Leeds) in 1952.

It was, in the light of these interests and his chairmanship of *Parish and People*, not surprising that Henry then became a founder-member of the Church of England Liturgical Commission in 1955. It was through this appointment that in due course he became a founder-member of the Joint Liturgical Group and, on that Group, the architect of the two-year thematic Sunday lectionary which, for a short time, bid fair to become a leader of the field ecumenically. It became part of the Church of England's 'alternative' provision when Series 3 Communion was authorized from February 1973, but was slowly overborne by the Roman Catholic three-year lectionary (and its ecumenical offspring, the 'Revised Common Lectionary'). The pressure was resisted and the thematic lectionary defended for the ASB in 1980, but external pressures also came upon the Church of England as other denominations and other Provinces of the Anglican Communion one-by-one went over to the 'RCL' in the subsequent years – and at the time of writing the de Candole two-year concept is in its twilight hour. But it happens to few both to lead a great proportion of the Church of England into a new broad shape of Sunday for half a century, and then in tandem with that change also to provide the Bible readings and themes which should mark that Parish Communion for nearly three decades.

He retired as suffragan bishop in 1965, but continued on the Commission (and thus saw his lectionary principles embedded in the Commission's programme) until 1969. As the author of this brief notice can witness from personal knowledge of him for the last six years of his life, he remained humble, cheerful, chubby-faced like a schoolboy (and he was also short in stature), and ever-enquiring in his mind right up to his last few months. He would never in those latter years have felt like the determined High Churchman of his youth, and his desire both to promote lay witness and the various lay roles in liturgy and to make the liturgy fully accessible to the worshippers is a measure of the move from his more-or-less doctrinaire, even old-fashioned, Catholicism in the 1920s to a wonderfully flexible concern for the pastoral usefulness of the liturgy by the 1960s. He moved naturally into the role of interpreting the scholars to the parishes, and moved easily among both, being loved and respected by both. He has found a useful, if slightly cautious biographer in Peter Jagger (*Bishop Henry de Candole – His Life and Times 1895–1971* (Faith Press, 1975)), and his personal history unites the frequently separate stories of leaders in the episcopate on the one hand, and the development of a liturgical movement in the Church of England on the other. Twenty-five years on, I still miss him.

SELECT BIBLIOGRAPHY

Being the Church Today: A Collection of Sermons and Addresses, Peter J. Jagger (ed.), Faith Press, 1974.

'The Calendar', R. C. D. Jasper (ed.), *The Calendar and Lectionary: A Reconsideration* (Joint Liturgical Group Publication), Oxford University Press, 1967.

The Christian Use of the Psalms, Mowbray, 1955.

The Church's Offering: A Brief Study of Eucharistic Worship, Mowbray, 1935.

The Church's Prayers, Mowbray, 1939.

The Church's Prayers: An Explanation of Mattins and Evensong, Mowbray, 1950.

(With Arthur Couratin) *Re-Shaping the Liturgy: Invitation to a Parish Enquiry* (Liturgical Commission booklet), CIO, 1964.

Common Prayer, Anglican Young People's Association series, SPCK, 1944.

'Giving and Receiving: Introduction', E. R. Morgan and Roger Lloyd (eds), *The Mission of the Anglican Communion*, SPCK, 1948.

Headings for the Lessons: for the Sundays and Principal Holy Days [in the Revised Table of Lessons]. Year 1, Mowbray, 1956.

Helps to Preaching at the Parish Communion, Mowbray, 1961.

'Instruction in Worship', A. G. Hebert (ed.), *The Parish Communion*, SPCK, 1937.

Peter J. Jagger, *Bishop Henry de Candole: His Life and Times 1895–1971*, Faith Press, 1975.

Lent with the Church: A Devotional Guide to the Liturgy of Lent, Mowbray, 1952.

'The Parish Communion after 25 Years', David M. Paton (ed.), *The Parish Communion To-day*, SPCK, 1962.

The Sacraments and the Church: A Study in the Corporate Nature of Christianity, Mowbray, 1935.

'The Study of Liturgiology', H. S. Box (ed.), *The Priest as Student*, SPCK, 1937.

14

E. C. R. LAMBURN

MARTIN DUDLEY

'The ceremonialists of a few years ago made a great mistake', wrote John Wickham Legg, 'in introducing the custom of placing six lights on the altar; it is a mistake, whether looked at from a legal, or historical, or politic, or aesthetic point of view. If we are to return to medieval ceremonial the six lights on the altar must be the first thing to be laid aside.' 'Two lights only upon the altar and never more than two is the use of the English Church today,' wrote the architect J. Ninian Comper, who served on the Alcuin Club committee with Legg in the first year, and added 'it was the universal use of Christendom until the thirteenth century.' Percy Dearmer agreed, though he thought that 'most parsons have set up this distinctively Roman Catholic feature in honest ignorance . . . But a mistake having been made, the most honest and manly course is to acknowledge and correct it.' The editors of *Ritual Notes* were unrepentant; they qualified the requirement for 'at least two candlesticks' by stating that 'it is usual, however, in accordance with rule and practice, for the high altar to be furnished with six – three on each side of the cross.'

The liturgiologists, Anglican and even Roman (Legg and Comper look to support from Edmund Bishop) might disagree; the traveller – Father Forse for example – might bring evidence of no candles, two or four candles, candles around the altar, candles on the screen, but for the devotees of *Ritual Notes*, 'a comprehensive guide to the Rites and Ceremonies of the Book of Common Prayer of the English Church interpreted in accordance with the latest revisions of the Western Use', six were needed, never less, often more. The 'big six', often gilded Florentine candlesticks on a gradine above the altar, were a clear mark of advanced Anglo-Catholicism. While Cyril Pocknee was at least partially correct when he anticipated that 'the row of six lights of modern Roman Catholic usage is likely to disappear as the liturgical revival spreads in the Latin rite', they have remained as a mark and badge.

Liturgical manuals describing services and ceremonies in great detail originated in eighteenth-century Italy, notably in Venice (Bauldry, Gavanti, Merati) and Rome (Catalani). They are detailed in their instructions and rich in historical notes. J. D. Hilarius Dale's *Ceremonies according to the Roman Rite*, a translation and adaptation of the manual by Baldeschi, appeared in 1853 (with further editions in 1859, 1873 and 1913). Adrian Fortescue wrote *Ceremonies of the Roman Rite* in 1917 to replace Dale, and it subsequently became known as Fortescue and O'Connell (8th edn 1947). Roman manuals influenced the Anglican manuals of the nineteenth century, the *Directorium Anglicanum* and Shipley's *Ritual of the Altar*. Antiquarian research into an appropriate English Use led to Dearmer's *The Parson's Handbook*, Staley's recommendations on ceremonial, the Alcuin Club's directories, and Spence's *An Anglican Use*. The most influential of the Western Use manuals for Anglicans, beginning from calendar notes on ordering services, was *Ritual Notes*, first edited in the 1890s by J. N. Burrows and W. Plimpton. The initials E. C. R. L. appear beneath the preface to the seventh edition of 1926. They belonged to Edward Cyril Russell Lamburn (1900–1979). He was involved in every subsequent edition and the eleventh, and last, edition (1964) carries his name alone on the cover and title page. Dearmer's *Handbook* was also very influential and reached its twelfth edition in 1932. It was reissued as a thirteenth edition, revised and rewritten by Pocknee, in 1965.

'There can be no doubt', wrote William Temple, Archbishop of York, in 1930, 'that the Church of England at present suffers very considerably from the great diversity in the outward appearance of its services as conducted by clergy of different schools of thought.' Temple did not want and certainly could not insist upon 'complete uniformity' in ceremonial but he wanted a sense that the variations were 'variants of one general scheme, so that any habitual worshipper in any of our churches will at once recognise and understand what is going on.' He concluded: 'If we are to reach such general agreement as I have indicated, it must be by a rather long process of experiment, and by a readiness to give up our own customs or attachments for the sake of the object in view.' The diversity of ceremonial practice was the product not merely of nineteenth-century ritualism but of the great number of manuals, more than one for each use or variant upon it. The more adventurous clergy supplemented their books with 'ecclesiological tours' that embraced the liturgical practice of France and Belgium, Italy and Spain.

E. C. R. Lamburn was born in 1900; he read theology, without distinction, at Worcester College, Oxford, was prepared for ordination at St Stephen's House, and ordained in the Diocese of London. He served his title at Christ Church, Clapton, and was then for twenty-five years at St Faith's, Cowes, on the Isle of Wight (1931–55) and seventeen years at Keyston with Bythorn, near Little Gidding (1955–72). After a period of retirement in Saffron Walden, he died on 30 May 1979. Little more is known of him than this, except that the Chapter Minutes record that when he retired in 1972 the clergy of his deanery (of which he was rural dean) paid tribute to his pastoral care both of his parishes and of his fellow clergy. His parishes do not seem to have enjoyed the advanced Catholic ceremonial he set down in his books. He compiled and edited, in addition to *Ritual Notes*, *Anglican Services* (1953 and 1963), *The Liturgy Develops* (1960), *Behind Rite and Ceremony* (1961) and two booklets concerned with the use of Series 2 (*Alternative Services: Using '1967': Some Notes*, 1968 and *Alternative Services: Using '1967' in Holy Week: Some Notes*, 1969).

It is in details and in conflicting advice and instructions that the real nature and influence of these books becomes clear. There is a difference in style. Dearmer and Pocknee are anxious to give historical notes and evidence for the practices they recommend or against those they deplore. Lamburn leaves all such corroboration to other works; his is a manual for liturgical celebration, prescriptive rather than exhortatory in style. Spence's manual, commended by William Temple, was not of the same lasting value as those of Lamburn and Dearmer, but he had attempted to substitute utility combined with reverence for doctrinal significance in ceremonial and rightly saw that the ceremonial controversy was really about the nature and authority of the Church of England.

There are conflicts between the Uses in exactly those areas one might have expected. A drawing of the altar showing the way of censing it was one of the distinctive features of *Ritual Notes*; Dearmer eschews such complicated procedures in the interests of simplicity – without the 'subtleties of double swings'. Pocknee expresses the aversion of 'many English people' to the elaborations of the modern Roman rite or the late medieval English usage in which the 'clinking of chains and the elaborate censings of persons and things are apt to occupy an undue prominence in the liturgy'. Lamburn allows lace as a decoration for the cotta and alb, at the cuffs and bottom or skirt. Dearmer simply states that the use of lace is 'not an English custom', while pointing out that the cotta is 'fortunately not one of the vestments ordered by our Rubric'. 'The biretta', Lamburn declares, 'is always worn by the celebrant of Mass.' Dearmer deplores the use of the Italian biretta, which 'offends an immense number of lay folk'. Pocknee thinks the biretta 'less comely' than the Canterbury cap. Dearmer and Pocknee are both opposed to genuflection as an act of reverence to the Blessed Sacrament; Lamburn prescribes it as the 'normal mark of reverence'.

Differing viewpoints are particularly evident when we look at seasonal observances. Clergy and parishes might have wanted a moderate form of 'English' ceremonial, but they increasingly wanted to observe a full liturgical round in Advent, at Christmas and in Holy Week, and Dearmer could not, or would not, give it to them. 'Experience leads one to doubt whether the revival of the Midnight Mass is desirable under modern conditions of life,' writes Dearmer, and Pocknee agreed (even in 1965!); Lamburn merely states 'It is proper to celebrate Mass at midnight on this festival. It should, if possible, be a high Mass . . .' Dearmer thinks that an enormous blaze of candles 'so long as the extra lights are not put on the altar itself' is the best way to observe Candlemas. Pocknee welcomes the blessing and procession of candles (using the Alcuin Club's rite). Lamburn requires the blessing and procession and insists on white vestments throughout. There are no ashes on Dearmer's Ash Wednesday nor on Pocknee's; Lamburn, of course, insists upon the blessing and distribution of ashes. Dearmer cannot, however, resist a Palm Sunday procession and falls back on the antiquarian principle that omission of old rites does not necessarily mean prohibition, but he has to fall back on the Sarum Missal for prayers, though Pocknee can refer again to the Alcuin Club. Lamburn expects the rite in the full form given by one of the English altar missals (such as Shipley's). Dearmer has no Good Friday 'creeping to the cross' and no Paschal candle. Pocknee encourages the Good Friday liturgy but has some reservations about the Paschal Vigil. Lamburn welcomes anything that Rome does and gives ample instruction to ensure that the rites are done properly and well. This was sufficient to encourage the use of *Ritual Notes* and its frequent revision.

Lamburn was alert to liturgical change and shows some sympathy with the 'wise modernity' of Pius XII, especially in his reform of Holy Week. These reforms would almost certainly have led to a thorough-going revision of the missal and breviary more obviously as a development rather than a replacement of the post-Tridentine liturgical books. Writing in the early 1960s, Lamburn was aware that church people were no longer content, as they had been, to be told what to do and how to do it. He was enthusiastic about the value of education and its relation to Christian practice. 'There is no credit', he wrote, 'in telling people to do this or that just because someone says they ought; if there is a rational basis, people should be told of it if they care to know; Christianity is not a routine carrying out of rites and ceremonies regardless of their rational basis.' In

Behind Rite and Ceremony he offered straightforward historical and liturgical explanations for the ceremonies, although he can be seen to slip from historical description into prescription in telling the reader how it should be done. Above all, he does not provide any arguments for adherence to the Roman rite. He appears to follow it blindly and the Roman missal and the Vatican's decrees are his constant companion. Even the liturgical reforms of the Second Vatican Council failed to undermine the value and significance of *Ritual Notes*. It is a necessary resource for those who want traditional Catholic worship and the eleventh edition has recently been republished.

One question remains. The study of liturgy in the late twentieth century has moved far from the vain attempt to establish an English Use. Concern for candles, two or six, double swings of the thurible, the wearing or not of birettas and inches of lace, is not shared by the modern liturgical scholar, and much of the elaborate ceremonial has been stripped out of the Western liturgies. Was the period of the manuals just the final flowering of a period of liturgical rigidity marked by absence of real creativity? I have never thought so. Lamburn explained that precise instructions, how to place the cruets, which way the gospel book should be placed, and so on, added to the dignity of worship and reduced ceremonial fussiness. He would have disagreed with Dearmer on an enormous number of ceremonial matters. However, he is likely to have agreed with the last lines of the preface to the second edition of *The Parson's Handbook*:

> If I had written a Cricketer's Handbook, no one would have complained of *minutiae*; if a Cookery Book, every one would have been up in arms against me for the superficial treatment of a great and serious subject. Yet I cannot help thinking that the worship of God calls for as careful treatment as the playing of games, and that an orderly complement of accessories is as necessary in the church as in the scullery.

SELECT BIBLIOGRAPHY

Alternative Services: Using '1967' in Holy Week: Some notes, W. Knott and Son, 1969.
Alternative Services: Using '1967': Some notes, W. Knott and Son, 1968.
Anglican Services, W. Knott and Son, 1953 and 1963.
Behind Rite and Ceremony, W. Knott and Son, 1961.
The Liturgy Develops, W. Knott and Son, 1960.
Ritual Notes, 7th edn, W. Knott and Son, 1926.

15

MASSEY H. SHEPHERD

RUTH MEYERS

In a *Festschrift* for Massey Shepherd, his colleague Sherman Johnson remarked, 'it is impossible to name another single person who has played a larger part in [the] development and acceptance [of the 1979 Book of Common Prayer]' ('Massey H. Shepherd and the Episcopal Church: A Reminiscence', in Burson (ed.), *Worship Points the Way*, p. 16). Responding to the Berakah Award given by the North American Academy of Liturgy in 1978, Shepherd commented, 'I . . . count myself fortunate by the grace of God to have lived, participated and agonized in a convulsive generation of liturgical reform such as the Church has not known since the sixteenth century.' But he regarded teaching as his greatest pleasure: 'None of my work . . . has been more rewarding or given me more joy than that of introducing year to year raw seminarians to the early church Fathers and the classic liturgies of the ancient Church' ('Berakah Award: Response', *Worship* 52 [1978]: 302).

Having earned his doctorate in church history at the University of Chicago, in 1940 Shepherd began teaching at Episcopal Theological School in Cambridge, Massachusetts, and in 1954 went to the Church Divinity School of the Pacific in Berkeley, California, where he remained until his retirement in 1981. Shepherd also shaped the thinking of the clergy who attended the Graduate School of Theology, a summer programme of the Episcopal seminary in Sewanee, Tennessee, which Shepherd directed from 1951 until 1970. At Sewanee under Shepherd's tutelage, many priests first learned of the

Liturgical Movement and considered how to introduce such renewal in their parishes.

Throughout his career, Shepherd maintained an interest in New Testament studies and Patristics. In addition to articles and book reviews, he contributed to the series 'Ecumenical Studies in Worship' a monograph entitled *The Paschal Liturgy and the Apocalypse*, a study of the origins and development of the paschal liturgy.

But Shepherd is best known for his contributions to liturgical renewal and prayer book revision in the Episcopal Church. After completing his doctorate in 1937, Shepherd visited Berkeley Divinity School in New Haven, Connecticut, where he was influenced by the Dean, William Palmer Ladd, a pioneer of the liturgical movement in the Episcopal Church. Shepherd had already discovered Romano Guardini's *The Spirit of the Liturgy* and Odo Casel's *Mysterientheologie*; at Berkeley he encountered a community and a mentor grappling with the practical implications of the Liturgical Movement.

To introduce Episcopalians to the ideals of the Liturgical Movement, Ladd had contributed a biweekly column, 'Prayer Book Interleaves', to the Episcopal Church periodical *The Witness*. After his death in 1941, the essays were published as a collection under the same title. Inspired by Ladd, Shepherd began a similar column, 'The Living Liturgy', and these essays likewise were published as a collection. Shepherd continued to contribute articles to popular Episcopal Church periodicals, thereby communicating to a wide audience the vision of the Liturgical Movement and its practical implications. He spoke at many clergy conferences and conducted numerous parish teaching missions. His scholarship was also placed at the service of the Church through *The Oxford American Prayer Book Commentary*, a survey of historical development and an interpretation of the rites of the 1928 prayer book, and *The Worship of the Church*, a volume in the [Episcopal] Church's Teaching Series intended for adult study. In both volumes Shepherd articulated the spirit of worship in the 1928 prayer book as viewed through the lens of the Liturgical Movement and contemporary liturgical scholarship.

Shepherd's passion for liturgical renewal is evident in his work with Associated Parishes, founded in 1946 by Shepherd and three other priests who wanted to implement the Liturgical Movement in their parishes and sought a place for accountability and support in their efforts. Associated Parishes became a principal organ of the Liturgical Movement in the Episcopal Church, and Shepherd's guiding hand was crucial to the organization in its first two decades. A co-founder, John Patterson, later credited Shepherd with continually recalling for members three basic principles: that Jesus Christ is Lord; that the Church is the earnest of Christ's kingdom; that the Eucharist is the great action of the Church. Grounded in these theological convictions, Associated Parishes endeavoured to renew the Church through the renewal of the liturgy.

To disseminate their ideals, Associated Parishes published a number of pamphlets during the 1950s. Most were published anonymously, but Shepherd's name appears as editor on two publications: a guide (published in 1956) to celebrating the Eucharist with the presider facing the people, and *Holy Week Offices* (1958), which drew primarily upon the Bible, the 1928 Prayer Book and the 1940 hymnal to supply rites not included in the Prayer Book.

Shepherd's active participation in Associated Parishes ceased after 1966, owing to his many other activities. In 1946 he had become a member of the Standing Liturgical Commission of the Episcopal Church, and after the death of Bayard Hale Jones in 1957, he was elected vice-chair, a position he held until his service on the commission concluded in 1976. In 1966 Shepherd was appointed as an observer to the Vatican Consilium for Implementation of the Constitution on the Sacred Liturgy, and that same year he became a member of the Commission on Worship of the Consultation on Church Union. Shepherd was also a co-founder of the Consultation on Common Texts. His contribution was a translation of psalms published in 1976 as *A Liturgical Psalter for the Eucharist.*

Participation in these ecumenical endeavours reflects Shepherd's perspective of the Liturgical Movement as an ecumenical ferment. In the Bohlen Lectures delivered in

Philadelphia in 1959 (published in 1961 as *The Reform of Liturgical Worship*), Shepherd was asked to discuss the Liturgical Movement in the context of the Episcopal Church, and he responded by tracing the history of liturgical renewal and revision in the Episcopal Church during the nineteenth and twentieth centuries. But he concluded with an ecumenical proposal, urging that the Episcopal Church work with Lutherans, Presbyterians and Methodists to produce a common eucharistic liturgy.

Notwithstanding his ecumenical interests, it was Prayer Book revision in the Episcopal Church, authorized by the 1967 General Convention, that consumed most of Shepherd's energy. A key element of the revision process was trial use, the use of proposed liturgical texts on a provisional basis. The Standing Liturgical Commission had unsuccessfully proposed to the triennial General Conventions in 1955 and 1958 an amendment to the Constitution of the Episcopal Church that would permit trial use. In 1961 the Commission published *The Problem and Method of Prayer Book Revision*, setting forth the rationale for trial use, and the General Convention that year took the unusual step of permitting Shepherd, who was not a deputy, to address the House of Deputies on the proposed amendment. Shepherd was persuasive; the amendment was approved by the 1961 convention, then adopted by the 1964 convention (the requisite process for amendments to the Constitution of the Episcopal Church).

Shepherd's contributions to Prayer Book revision predate his service on the Standing Liturgical Commission. In 1945 he was invited to help draft a revision of the 1928 baptismal rite. This was eventually published in 1951 as the first of a series of 'Prayer Book Studies', presented by the Standing Liturgical Commission for study and discussion. A conservative revision, *Prayer Book Studies I: Baptism and Confirmation* (New York: Church Hymnal Corporation) leaned heavily toward the Mason-Dix theology of initiation. Explicit references to the gift of the Holy Spirit in baptism were absent, and the introduction to the study equivocated in discussing the work of the Spirit in baptism. Shepherd's work in his Prayer Book commentary and in the Church's Teaching Series, published a year after *Prayer Book Studies I*, suggests that he viewed confirmation as the completion of Christian initiation and a bestowal of the indwelling gifts of the Spirit, although he also recognized the Spirit's agency in the new birth of baptism.

In 1959 Shepherd told the Standing Liturgical Commission that his position on confirmation had changed. Although the commission asked him to consider further revisions of the initiatory rites, he did not have the time to do so. However, in the Bradner Lectures delivered at General Theological Seminary in 1964 (published as *Liturgy and Education*), he proposed that baptism, confirmation and admission to communion be reintegrated in a single rite administered by the bishop. By coincidence, the Standing Liturgical Commission was meeting at General Seminary and attended Shepherd's lecture. Thus he helped influence their thinking on Christian initiation even though he did not serve on the drafting committee which developed the initiatory rites for the 1979 Prayer Book.

Shepherd's major contribution to the 1979 Prayer Book was the calendar and the eucharistic lectionary. He served on the subcommittee on the calendar which in 1957 proposed a revised calendar with 92 black-letter days – lesser festivals in the Church's calendar – followed in 1958 by propers for those days. Much of the initial work had been done by Bayard Jones before his death, but Shepherd edited Jones's work and contributed a section on Lenten weekday propers. This was a significant enrichment for the Episcopal Church, which prior to that time had not included black-letter days on its liturgical calendar.

In addition to the calendar of lesser feasts, Shepherd chaired the Drafting Committee on the Calendar, Eucharistic Lectionary, and Collects throughout the period of prayer book revision. He brought to the Episcopal Church the three-year cycle of lections introduced in the Roman Catholic Church in 1969, a development of which he learned in his role as observer to the Roman Catholic Consilium.

After the three-year lectionary had been adopted in several denominations, Shepherd became an advocate of a common lectionary, which he believed could be an invaluable means of promoting unity in faith and witness. To that end, under the auspices of the Consultation on Common Texts, he convened a 1978 conference to assess the lectionary and its adaptations. The conference resulted in the formation of the North American Committee on Calendar and Lectionary, which in 1983 published the *Common Lectionary*. While Shepherd did not serve on the Committee, he helped provide the impetus for its work.

Shepherd's influence extends far beyond the calendar and lectionary. A senior scholar at the time of Prayer Book revision, Shepherd's opinion carried significant weight. For example, he opposed the inclusion of a reference to the flood in the newly written Thanksgiving over the Water at baptism, and the phrase was deleted. He is credited with writing thirteen collects, the Litany of Penitence in the Ash Wednesday liturgy, the Litany of Thanksgiving for optional use on Thanksgiving Day, and three postcommunion prayers.

Shepherd also did much to encourage acceptance of the new Prayer Book. Not only did he travel extensively to introduce new rites, he served as chaplain to the House of Deputies at the General Conventions in 1969, 1970, 1973 and 1976. John Coburn, president of the House of Deputies during those years, comments that through Shepherd's humble service as chaplain, the Deputies 'were increasingly bound together by a sense of common purpose deepened by the conviction that the spirit who moved among them was God's own Holy Spirit' ('The Prayers of Massey Shepherd as Chaplain to the House of Deputies', in Burson (ed.), *Worship Points the Way*, p. 27). In so many ways, Shepherd's scholarship and leadership were crucial in the development and acceptance of the 1979 Prayer Book.

SELECT BIBLIOGRAPHY

'Berakah Award: Response', *Worship* 52, 1978, p. 302.

Holy Week Offices, Seabury Press, 1958.

The Liturgical Movement and the Prayer Book, Seabury Press/Western Theological Seminary, 1946.

Liturgy and Education, Oxford University Press, 1965.

The Living Liturgy, Oxford University Press, 1946.

The Oxford American Prayer Book Commentary, Oxford University Press, 1950.

The Paschal Liturgy and the Apocalypse, Ecumenical Studies in Worship 6, John Knox Press/Lutterworth Press, 1960.

Prayer Book Studies I: Baptism and Confirmation, Church Hymnal Corporation, 1951.

The Reform of Liturgical Worship: Perspectives and Prospects, Oxford University Press, 1961.

The Worship of the Church, The Church's Teaching Series, vol. 4, Seabury Press, 1952.

A more complete Bibliography may be found in Malcolm C. Bursen (ed.), *Worship Points the Way: A Celebration of the Life and Work of Massey H. Shepherd, Jr.*, Seabury Press, 1981, pp. 273–83.

16

GREGORY DIX

PAUL BRADSHAW

Of all Anglican liturgical scholars, Gregory Dix (1901–1952) is unquestionably the one who has exercised the greatest influence not only within the Anglican Communion but also outside it. A monk of the Benedictine Abbey at Nashdom from 1936 until his death, his contributions to scholarship cover a wide range of topics, but his most enduring effects have been felt in three areas – the *Apostolic Tradition* of Hippolytus, confirmation, and above all the Eucharist.

THE APOSTOLIC TRADITION OF HIPPOLYTUS

Although several scholars had preceded Dix in producing reconstructions of what was thought to be the original text of this enigmatic ancient church order, attributed to the third-century Hippolytus of Rome by Eduard Schwartz and R. H. Connolly early in the twentieth century, Dix was the first to attempt a critical edition with a complete scholarly *apparatus criticus*. Published in 1937 by SPCK, he intended it to be the first of two volumes; the second (which never appeared) was to contain a 'detailed Introduction and all consideration of the book's contents and setting'. Although for serious students it was superseded by a superior French edition of the text made by Bernard Botte in 1963, it has continued to be widely used by English-speaking readers, and was reissued in a second edition with preface and corrections by Henry Chadwick in 1968.

Many of Dix's conclusions about the correct reading of the

text have been supported by subsequent scholars, but at a number of points he made decisions based less on the value of the textual evidence itself than on his own convictions about what must have been the case in the third-century Church. Perhaps the most contentious of these was in the prayer that accompanies the post-baptismal imposition of hands (which Dix labels confidently as 'confirmation'). Here he disregarded the testimony of the Latin version (to which elsewhere in the document he assigned great weight) in favour of the oriental-language witnesses, because the former associated the gift of the Holy Spirit with the baptism that had already been received while the latter prayed for its descent upon the newly baptized.

In the long run, Dix's reconstruction of the text of this church order is unlikely to stand, and even his judgement on its author, date, and provenance, which he shares in common with many other leading scholars, may not survive the challenges being mounted by some critics today. But he will always be revered as a trail-blazer in the recovery of this most crucial of ancient Christian documents, which has exercised such a pervasive influence on liturgical revision in the second half of the twentieth century.

CONFIRMATION

Dix's forays into the traditional Anglican battleground over the meaning and importance of the rite of confirmation came chiefly in two monographs, *Confirmation or The Laying on of Hands?* (SPCK, London, 1936) and *The Theology of Confirmation in relation to Baptism* (London, Dacre, 1946). He argued that confirmation had constituted the essential second half of Christian initiation from New Testament times onwards (water baptism being the first); that it had at first consisted of an anointing with oil and had originated as the Christian equivalent of Jewish circumcision; and that it conveyed the gift of the Holy Spirit, being what patristic writers were referring to when they spoke of 'sealing'. He thus stood firmly in the Catholic tradition within Anglicanism, and because his position on this subject coincided to a considerable extent with that of an earlier writer, A. J. Mason, it is often humourously described as 'the Mason-Dix line'.

His interpretation of the historical evidence was challenged at the time by the more Protestant scholar Geoffrey Lampe in his book *The Seal of the Spirit* (London, SPCK, 1951; 2nd edn 1967), and more recent research would undermine Dix's arguments still further. He simply tried to claim too much for confirmation from the biblical and Patristic evidence. Yet, on the positive side, his efforts, and those of like-minded theologians, did help ensure that the Church of England did not slide uncritically into the view that water-baptism was the only thing that mattered in the process of Christian initiation. Whatever may have been the practice in New Testament times – and the evidence is too meagre for a safe conclusion to be reached on that question – it is clear that in the Christianity of the next few centuries the rites of initiation always involved a complex cluster of closely related ceremonies, even though these may have varied in their form and meaning from region to region and period to period.

EUCHARIST

Among Dix's various contributions to the subject of the Eucharist, pride of place has obviously to go to his massive work, *The Shape of the Liturgy* (London, Dacre, 1945). Against the background of earlier scholarship that had mostly tried to find an original apostolic eucharistic rite in the assorted bits of evidence that survive from the first few centuries of Christianity's existence, Dix asserted that the common root of the varied later forms of the Eucharist was to be found not in a complete rite as such but in their underlying structure:

> What was fixed and immutable everywhere in the second century was the outline or Shape of the Liturgy, what was *done*. What our Lord instituted was not a 'service', something said, but an action, something done – or rather the continuation of a traditional Jewish action, but with a new meaning . . . (*op. cit.*, pp. 214–15)

Dix argued that the New Testament accounts of the Last Supper reveal this action as originally having a sevenfold shape – taking bread, giving thanks over it, breaking it, and sharing it; and then after the meal, taking a cup of wine, giving thanks over it, and sharing it – but that 'with absolute unanimity' the early liturgical tradition condensed this to a fourfold shape – taking bread and cup together, giving thanks over them, breaking the bread, and distributing both. It was only the gradual overlaying of this fundamental pattern with later strata that had obscured it in the developed eucharistic rites of East and West.

There was much more than this in the book, but it was this basic thesis that won universal acceptance among later generations of liturgical scholars from many Christian denominations. A considerable number may have disputed Dix's identification of the 'taking' with the bringing up of the eucharistic elements to the president (i.e. the offertory procession) rather than with the president's taking of them into his hands in order to say the thanksgiving over them, but until very recently it would have been virtually impossible to find a serious scholar who did not accept the assumption that all early Christian eucharistic rites were built upon the foundation of the four-action shape. Consequently, when the revision of eucharistic rites and texts began in the second half of the twentieth century, the marks of this perspective can be seen to varying degrees in almost every new or modified form that has emerged out of this process in all the mainstream Christian churches.

The latest scholarship, however, would be somewhat more cautious than Dix about the form of the primitive Christian Eucharist. Some would judge that to speak of a four-action shape is to give undue emphasis to actions that are essentially subordinate, and that it is really a two-action shape – thanking and sharing: we take only in order to thank, we break only in order to share. A few would go further still and question the universality of even this pattern in early Christianity, suggesting that Eucharists without wine and Eucharists with the order cup–bread rather than bread–cup may have been more common than has usually been supposed.

Among other themes developed in the book, two in particular may be mentioned as having strongly influenced later thinking about the Eucharist: the importance of 'anamnesis' and of eschatology. Dix insisted that

> in the scriptures both of the Old and New Testament, *anamnesis* and the cognate verb have the sense of 're-calling' or 're-presenting' before God an event in the past, so that it becomes *here and now operative by its effects*. (*op. cit.*, p. 161, emphasis in original)

The significance of this term was also stressed by the biblical scholar Joachim Jeremias (although with a somewhat different understanding), and it was taken up by the French Protestant theologian Max Thurian. It was he who was chiefly responsible for its entry into the arena of ecumenical discussion, where it has proved to be a valuable mediating concept between classical Catholic and Protestant interpretations of the Eucharist. Thus the Agreed Statement on the Eucharist of the Anglican-Roman Catholic International Commission affirms that

> the notion of *memorial* as understood in the passover celebration at the time of Christ – i.e. the making effective in the present of an event in the past – has opened the way to a clearer understanding of the relationship between Christ's sacrifice and the eucharist. The eucharistic memorial is no mere calling to mind of a past event or of its significance, but the church's effectual proclamation of God's mighty acts.

Dix's emphasis on the part that eschatology played in shaping early Christian worship has also been enthusiastically received. At the same time, however, his over-simple distinction between what he saw as the essentially eschatological character of the worship of the ante-Nicene period and the focus on historical commemoration in the post-Nicene era has come under challenge from more recent scholarship: there are certainly some differences between the two periods, but they cannot be contrasted as sharply as Dix tried to do.

As this brief survey reveals, Dix's interests were never

purely academic. His liturgical study was always historical scholarship at the service of the Church. This was both its strength and its weakness. What he tried to do was to show how knowledge of the past, and especially of the early Church, had a part to play in the practice and theology of the present, not so much because he was a 'patristic fundamentalist' longing to turn the clock back to the Golden Age (though there are certainly elements of this in his writings), but because he believed in the vital importance of tradition for the Christian faith. The danger that this brought, however, was that on various occasions he saw in the past what he wanted to find there and not necessarily what the sources themselves would support. The triumph of theory over evidence is, of course, something from which no scholar is immune. But the consequences for those of us who are also engaged in helping shape the liturgical practices of the Church of our own day can be far more pernicious than they are for the ivory-towered academic.

Dix's legacy to the future, therefore, will be not so much his technical historical research, which has already been superseded at many points, but his theology of liturgy, his vision of what Christian liturgy should be: the action of the whole people of God under the presidency of its bishop and clergy. Many others have written along similar lines – it was for example the vision that underlay the Anglican 'Parish Communion Movement' (see Gabriel Hebert (ed.), *The Parish Communion* (London, SPCK, 1937), to which Dix himself contributed an essay) as well as the Roman Catholic Constitution on the Sacred Liturgy of the Second Vatican Council promulgated in 1963 (see especially paras. 26ff.) – but none have articulated it better or more influentially than Dom Gregory Dix.

SELECT BIBLIOGRAPHY

The Apostolic Tradition of Hippolytus, SPCK, 1937.
Confirmation or The Laying on of Hands?, SPCK, 1936.
The Shape of the Liturgy, Dacre, 1945.
The Theology of Confirmation in Relation to Baptism, Dacre, 1946.

A full list of Dix's publications in chronological order can be found in Kenneth W. Stevenson, *Gregory Dix – Twenty-Five Years on*, Grove Liturgical Study No. 10, Grove Books, 1977, Appendix 2, and in Simon Bailey, *A Tactful God: Gregory Dix, Priest, Monk, and Scholar*, Gracewing, 1995, Appendix I.

17

ARTHUR COURATIN

RICHARD BUXTON

Perhaps I had better begin this attempt to assess the liturgical legacy of Arthur Couratin on a personal note, for what I have written is very much an appreciation from a personal standpoint, and one which I am aware, as I put pen to paper, that in places some may wish to disagree with strongly. I write as an Anglican priest, who sees himself firmly within the Catholic tradition of Anglicanism, trained at St Stephen's House, the theological college of which Arthur Couratin was Principal and which he so dominated for a quarter of a century, but not trained by him. I went up there in 1965, three years after he had left.

In point of fact I never met him, and so I am dependent for this on his published work and on the reminiscences of others. Because he was a larger than life character, the latter are legion. The former is rather sparser, for he published relatively little, apart from a multitude of book reviews.

No biography of him has been written to date, but Bryan Spinks and Michael Melrose wrote very brief appreciations of him some years ago in the Preface and Biographical note affixed to the *Festschrift* that Bryan Spinks edited in his honour, *The Sacrifice of Praise*. Michael Melrose also compiled a bibliography of his writings which was published in the same volume.

This brief account of his contributions to liturgy must perforce confine itself to a series of largely impressionistic sketches, under the five headings of his scholarship, teaching, contribution to liturgical revision, his own liturgical style and his advice to others on such practical matters.

His life was a long one. Born in 1902, he died at the age of 86 in 1988, though his illness in 1972 largely brought his scholarly career to an end at that time. His knowledge of liturgy was magisterial and profound, but his interests and viewpoints were tailored in directions which he largely shared with Edward Ratcliff, whose influence certainly helped to formulate his own mind, as he gladly acknowledged. As Michael Melrose expressed it, 'an abiding interest in the early Western, or rather Romano-African tradition, a slight distaste for what lay further east'. He was not overly sympathetic to the theological tradition of the English Book of Common Prayer, but as a teacher of liturgy to English ordinands he was concerned that they should properly understand it.

The area of fundamental liturgical scholarship of greatest interest to him was the origins and development of the eucharistic prayer, and he assembled much material in this field. He brought a necessary correction to Dix's ideas about the four-action shape, by expounding offertory and fraction as properly subordinate to the eucharistic prayer and communion respectively. Sufficient of his writings about the eucharistic prayer survive in fragmentary form to show the quality of scholarship of which he was capable, but he never worked it up into a major piece of published work.

But perhaps his greatest contribution to liturgy lay in his gifts as a teacher and popular communicator. He was by all accounts a brilliant lecturer and teacher of the subject, with a host of witty and memorable aphorisms to make his points. His remark about the apostolic succession being a matter of bottoms on thrones rather than hands on heads is perhaps one of the best known, but there are many more; space forbids any attempt at extensive quotation here.

And some of his most effective writing comes under the heading of teaching and communication. One thinks of his contribution to *The Pelican Guide to Modern Theology* (1969) where in just over one hundred succinct pages a masterly summary is given of baptism and eucharist liturgy from their origins up to the time at which he wrote, a near impossible task as he acknowledged in his final paragraph, but no one could have done it better, and most not nearly as well. Also there is *Reshaping the Liturgy*, which he wrote with Henry de Candole in 1964, at the dawn of the era of modern liturgical change in the Church of England. The aim of this pamphlet of about forty pages in length is to introduce parishes to the whole question of the revision of the Communion Service, both rite and praxis, with many questions for discussion to aid the process.

This leads naturally to a consideration of his contribution to the actual process of liturgical revision in England and Wales. He was a member of the original English Liturgical Commission that started the whole process of liturgical revision, and composition *ab initio*, or as near to *ab initio* as any denomination with an independent history of four hundred years can hope to achieve, that led to the *Alternative Service Book* of 1980. He was largely responsible for the early drafts of the new baptism and confirmation services and also for the Series 2 order of Holy Communion. With regard to the communion service, that this commission could start with the assumption that it was providing a eucharistic rite for a Parish Communion style of worship, which it did without challenge from anywhere, is in itself witness to how the liturgical life of the Church of England had changed in the previous twenty years. He left the commission because of profound disagreement with the outcome of the debate about the anamnesis paragraph in the eucharistic prayer of Series 2. He had wanted the wording of the prayer to offer the bread and wine to God, holding this to be the universal practice of antiquity, but the composition and political processes of the Church of England made this impossible to achieve. Perhaps he was naive to assume that it would be possible to return directly to antiquity in this respect, simply bypassing the effects of the Middle Ages, when the use of sacrificial language in the eucharistic prayer acquired overtones quite unacceptable to very many in the Church of England, and which it had not had in the Patristic era. He was left lamenting of Series 2 that 'it stands firmly outside the main tradition of Christian antiquity and of the modern Greek and Latin Churches'.

He played a leading part in the Church of Wales too, in the process of revision that led to the production of the interim eucharistic rite of 1966, which was incorporated with minimal change into the 1984 Welsh Book of Common Prayer. In his lecture to the Liturgical Conference at Carmarthen in 1965, citing antiquity, he argued that the Memorial of Christ is made 'by offering the Bread and the Cup to God'. The anamnesis in the Welsh rite does not use the word 'offer', but it does say 'we thy servants, with all thy holy people, do set forth before the Divine Majesty this Bread of eternal life and this Cup of everlasting salvation'. Arguably this is synonymous with offering, as well as being an almost direct, and evocatively beautiful, quotation from the Roman Canon. I think he must have been satisfied with this outcome, and indeed perhaps this Welsh rite is the most lasting practical memorial to his liturgical work.

As a footnote, it is interesting to note that the eucharistic rite produced by the Commission of the Covenanted Churches in Wales does say in its anamnesis paragraph 'we offer to you these your gifts of bread and wine', an ironic comment on the nervousness that Anglicans in this country (at least those who live south of Hadrian's Wall) have of using 'offer' at this point in the Eucharist, in contrast to some of their Reformed Brethren. I think this is an irony he would have appreciated.

It was also important to him that this followed the institution narrative, on which he held to the Latin doctrine that it constituted the moment of consecration. In this he doubtless shared Ratcliff's view that this was and always had been the doctrine of the English Prayer Book tradition, another point on which scholarship has moved on since his day.

With regard to his liturgical style, this was notable for sobriety and directness. There is no doubt he shared Edmund Bishop's view of the Roman Rite that its essential characteristics were 'soberness and sense', and based his own liturgical practice upon these precepts. He was eirenic in his approach to the variety of ceremonial tradition in the Church of England. It has been said of him: 'he might well celebrate at a north end parish with scarf and hood at 8.00 a.m. and then at 11 a.m. be at a High Mass with all the pre-Vatican II trimmings'. Within St Stephen's House itself, he ensured that its liturgical life was firmly based around the services of the 1662 *Book of Common Prayer* (the new authorized services did not begin to appear until after he had left) – 'This is an Anglican theological college; we do not have Roman Catholic services here', he is once reputed to have said. There was plainsong for the offices, and an essentially sober Latin ceremonial at the Mass. He moved the House from a tradition of priests on the staff serving each other's masses to one of concelebration. Whether the modern form of concelebration really is a true revival of an ancient practice, or something that merely looks like one devised to suit a modern (passing?) need is perhaps debatable, but it is certainly an improvement on what went before it.

He had a considerable effect on the liturgical life of Durham Cathedral when he went there as a residentiary canon after leaving St Stephen's House. Finding Matins was still the main morning service when he got there, he persuaded the chapter to introduce in addition a Sung Eucharist, devised a simple and dignified ritual to accompany it, and oversaw the purchase of chasubles, dalmatics and copes in the four liturgical colours for it.

He also knew that good liturgical presidential style had to be taught and learned, and his students at St Stephen's House were subjected to rigorous and immensely practical sessions on how Mass should be celebrated. His tuition concerning the – then very new – custom of celebrating westward facing gave rise to another of his celebrated aphorisms. When celebrating from behind the altar one should not genuflect, he maintained, lest the congregation be given the impression they are looking at the head of John the Baptist on a platter. By today's standards his tuition was rather regimented and according to the drill book, but the much freer styles of presidency we are now used to place more not fewer demands on the skill and knowledge of the celebrant, and the Church would do well to follow him in recognizing the need for good and thorough instruction of clergy and ordinands in this area.

A good number of people turned to him for practical liturgical advice, not least many bishops. Most notable among these, perhaps, was Kenneth Kirk, Bishop of Oxford, upon whom, it has been hinted, he exercised something of a restraining influence in matters ceremonial.

Is it possible to summarize his achievement in a sentence or two? Is Peter Cobb's assessment fair? He wrote of him (in the brief history of St Stephen's House published in 1976): 'His first love was liturgy and, although he was perhaps not very original himself, he adopted and disseminated the ideas of his friends E. C. Ratcliff and Gregory Dix to innumerable students.' He was certainly a man of great learning, and widely influential in many positive ways, and if the legacy of his original writing is small, perhaps this is due to a certain proper modesty in the face of some of the seemingly intractable problems of scholarship that investigation of the early history of the liturgy throws up. One of his major contributions was his many valuable and incisive book reviews; perhaps it would be worthwhile to collect many of these together and republish them in a single volume. As a footnote, I would add that writing this essay makes me realize just how much liturgical scholarship has moved on in the last twenty-five years. What is absolutely certain is that Arthur Couratin was a quite brilliant teacher of the subject.

But is this the final word that has to be said about him? I fear not, for perhaps in the last analysis one has to say that Arthur Couratin was one of those people, the combined effect of whose great faith and devotion to the Catholic wing of Anglicanism was to lead it further up the cul-de-sac entered by those Anglo-Catholics of the nineteenth century who took as their model the Latin mind-set of the contemporary Roman Church. From this blind alley sections of Anglicanism cannot now escape because of their tragic inability to accept God's call to women at the end of the second millennium to participate fully in all aspects of the ministerial life of the Church. This looks likely to reduce considerable sections of the Catholic wing of Anglicanism to a declining and ineffectual rump, and denies the rest of Anglicanism the very necessary witness and nourishment that a Catholic and sacramental approach to worship gives to those who participate in it, all of which will impoverish and stultify the life of the whole Anglican Communion. It also removes one of the counterbalances to Roman Catholic distortions of Catholicism. That such a life of valuable well-appreciated scholarship, faith and devotion should have contributed to such an outcome is very sad.

But whatever view is taken of Arthur Couratin, he was a powerful and influential figure in twentieth-century Anglicanism. I stated at the beginning of this essay that his biography has not yet been written. Perhaps it should be.

SELECT BIBLIOGRAPHY

With Henry de Candole, *Reshaping the Liturgy*, Church Information Office, 1964.

'Justin Martyr and Confirmation – a Note', *Theology*, vol. 55, 1952.

'Liturgiology 1939–1960', *Theology*, vol. 63, 1960.

'Liturgy', *The Pelican Guide to Modern Theology*, vol. 2, 1969.

'Revising the Eucharist', *The Liturgical Congress at Carmarthen*, Church in Wales Publications, 1965.

'The Sanctus and the Pattern of the Anaphora. A note on the Roman Sanctus', *Journal of Ecclesiastical History*, vol. 2, 1951.

'The Service of Holy Communion 1552–1662', *Church Quarterly Review*, vol. 163, 1962.

'Thanksgiving and Thankoffering', *Studia Liturgica*, vol. 3, 1964.

'The Tradition Received: We offer this bread and this cup' (number 2 in a group of four articles), *Theology*, vol. 69, 1966.

An extensive bibliography was compiled by Michael Melrose and is to be found in Bryan D. Spinks (ed.), *The Sacrifice of Praise: Studies on the themes of thanksgiving and redemption in the central prayers of the eucharistic and baptismal liturgies – in honour of Arthur Hubert Couratin*, CLV Edizioni Liturgiche, 1981.

18

C. E. POCKNEE

MARTIN DUDLEY

Born in 1906, Cyril Edward Pocknee studied theology at King's College, London, where Percy Dearmer was Professor of Ecclesiastical Art. Ordained in 1934, Pocknee served a number of curacies in Southwark diocese, then became Rector of Taverham (1939–43), curate of Hayes (1943–45), Vicar of St Mary, Edmonton (1946–55) and finally Vicar of Holy Trinity, Twickenham (1955–72). He retired to Ramsgate and died on 15 July 1979.

He wrote a number of books. His first was Alcuin Club Tract XXIX, published in 1954. It was a study entitled *The French Diocesan Hymns and Their Melodies*. It seemed an unlikely subject for a tract, but some fifty of the Neo-Gallican hymns from the revised breviaries and missals produced in the French Church under Louis XIV made their way, in translation, into English hymnals, and Pocknee provides, after an historical introduction, the full Latin text and a translation of those hymns, together with some musical illustrations. Pocknee believed that it was the Tractarians who sought out Latin office hymns but that they failed to distinguish between the truly ancient ones and the relatively modern compositions of the French breviaries until John Mason Neale pointed out the clear difference between them.

The Alcuin Club subsequently published three important illustrated volumes by Pocknee: *Liturgical Vesture: Its Origins and Development* (1960), *Cross and Crucifix In Christian Worship and Devotion* (1962), and *The Christian Altar In History and Today* (1963). His study of baptism and confirmation, *The Rites of Christian Initiation* (which I have not seen), appeared in 1962, as those rites were being revised for Series 2. Pocknee's final achievement was his revision of Dearmer's *The Parson's Handbook* which appeared, as the 13th edition, in 1965.

Pocknee provides us with considerable insight into his character and concerns in the long introduction to *The Parson's Handbook* and in the more personal parts of other books. He saw himself standing in clear succession to the founder-members of the Alcuin Club, in their loyalty to the Book of Common Prayer and to the Church of England as both Catholic and Reformed. He shared with them a belief that the English Prayer Book had 'Catholic rites and ceremonies which did not require to be supplemented by additions and borrowings from the Roman Missal'. Pocknee followed on from W. H. Frere, Charles Gore, W. H. St John Hope, J. Wickham Legg, Francis Eeles, Jocelyn Perkins, A. S. Duncan-Jones, J. H. Arnold and, of course, Percy Dearmer. Dearmer was the popularizer who took the researches of the 'antiquarians and liturgiologists' and made them available to the clergy. Pocknee carries on this work, and the introduction advances the question of 'English Use' and reviews the significant literature: Gabriel Hebert's *Liturgy and Society* and *The Parish Communion*, Dix's *The Shape of the Liturgy* and, most significantly of all, Joseph Jungmann's *The Mass of the Roman Rite*. But Pocknee is also concerned with more pressing and practical issues – the furnishings and ornaments of the church, the maintenance of the building and the granting of faculties that are in line with the best thinking on liturgy, and the state of church music. Initially, there seems to be a broadness and generosity of spirit in Pocknee's writing. Some of the issues addressed by Legg, Staley and Dearmer are, he sees, no longer significant; some of the positions they held are now untenable. However, like so many liturgical writers, Pocknee cannot help being prescriptive and his onslaught on brass as 'a vulgar and tawdry substitute for gold' and on the 'particularly hideous form of bulbous brass flower vase' is worthy of his noble, and acerbic, predecessors.

Like these predecessors, Pocknee wanted to establish, even in the 1960s, what was allowed by the Ornaments Rubric. In the introduction to *Liturgical Vesture* he stressed that the revival of the use of the alb (he insists on the spelling 'albe') and chasuble corresponds with the 'recovery of the Holy Eucharist as the chief act of Christian worship brought about by the Oxford movement last century'. In reviving the use the priests were not reviving medievalism but doing 'what the rest of Christendom has never ceased to do, that is, to give the Lord's own Service its rightful place as the central act of worship'. While fully supporting the return to traditional eucharistic vesture, Pocknee also supports the surplice against its detractors in every century. He mocks the idea that the chasuble is Catholic and the surplice Protestant, for the latter is of medieval origin and is associated with monastic choir offices. He concludes that 'the use of the surplice as a symbol of a reformed and primitive Christianity is a modern innovation, and does not even find support in the Reformation period'. His historical accounts of the origin of the various vestments are objective and informative, but he cannot help, in the best traditions of Legg and Staley, criticism of, for example, the 'effeminate custom' of using lace for the skirt cuffs of albs and the replacing of the surplice by the attenuated and square-yoked cotta. The Roman Catholic Church comes in for a good deal of criticism for it is marked by the 'general degradation of liturgical vesture that reached its nadir in the later baroque and rococo periods'.

Cross and Crucifix has no polemical intent; it is a good illustrated survey of the development of different forms of this essential Christian sign. In *The Christian Altar* Pocknee returns to the fray and is again both critical of prevailing practice and prescriptive. It is true that there was much to complain of. The cube-shaped altar, popularized by the Liturgical Movement, needs to be, and rarely is, surmounted by a ciborium if it is not to appear mean and insignificant. The controversy over the number of candles can, he thinks, be laid to rest for the 'argument that six is more correct and catholic than two is now an outmoded controversy'. The altar cross 'is a very late innovation and only since the second phase of the Oxford Movement has it come to be assumed, quite mistakenly, that *all* altars must have a cross of some kind standing on them'.

The worst possible criticism of any liturgical practice is to call it a 'very late' or 'modern innovation'. 'Cut flowers in vases form no part of the appointments of the Christian altar.' This rather niggardly approach can be disconcerting but when Pocknee gets into his stride he is always worth heeding:

> The last three decades have witnessed a growing revolt in church design and architecture against mere revivalism and the copying of the past. It is asserted that we must produce works of art for use in Christian worship which are modern and contemporary. These assertions will command widespread assent; but they can become dangerous clichés when applied to the design of the Christian altar and its surroundings. What is contemporary today can easily be outmoded tomorrow if the function of the church is not understood by our architects, as it appears not to be in more than one so-called modern design for a church. Moreover, in Christian worship and its art the element of tradition cannot be entirely eliminated or ignored, since tradition is based on the wisdom and experience of the past and not simply on conservatism. The desire to be up-to-date and contemporary in worship and in the planning of the altar and its setting can easily lead to the production of something which in striving to be different is merely grotesque and bizarre. Indeed, it can even produce something unfunctional when the fundamental traditions of the altar and its surroundings are laid aside for the sake of novelty of effect.

It was the increasing lack of respect for the tradition, even when it carried practical wisdom and the fruit of liturgical experience, that brought Pocknee to his last work. The dust jacket briefly summarized the reasons for a new edition of *The Parson's Handbook* after 33 years. Dearmer's work commanded respect and his careful directions for the whole conduct of Anglican worship had a lasting value and influence. Much of what Dearmer objected to had died out and his writing was too prolix for modern taste. So Pocknee revised it and his revision was admirable. It reduced the book from over five hundred pages to a manageable two hundred by omitting Dearmer's long evidences in support of this or that position.

Pocknee's main failure – the marked tendency to be didactic and prescriptive which was such an obvious failing of the whole school of antiquarian liturgists – is much in evidence, but he had an undeniable sense of what constituted good liturgical practice and was not afraid to give it voice. There are many areas in which he still needs to be heard. Here are some examples:

- Anglican worship tends to be too static and anything that can bring ordered and purposeful movement into it is to be welcomed.
- There is too much noisy and rather trite music being performed in our churches.
- The fear of colour in our churches still lingers in the minds of many English people.
- The use of 'electric' candles is contrary to the mind of the Church.
- Lamps may be hung before altars; electric light should not be used in such lamps.
- The desire to multiply crosses on and around the Holy Table should be resisted.
- Altar rails form no part of the traditional furniture of the sanctuary.
- The chancel should not be crowded with desks and benches.
- It is a mistake to encumber the chancel with a special chair for the bishop.
- Ferns and pots of flowers must not be stood in the font.
- The Offices of Matins and Evensong should not be prefaced by the lusty singing of a hymn.
- The blessing at Matins and Evensong should not be followed by a hymn or recessional.
- The bishop's pastoral staff is an ensign of office and not one of mere jurisdiction; all bishops may carry a staff when in episcopal vesture.
- There is no significance in placing an empty chalice and paten on the altar at the beginning of the Eucharist and

covering them with a coloured silk veil; 'this kind of thing is a meaningless ceremony'.
- The bread given at the Eucharist ought to be really broken and shared.

Perhaps the most glorious piece of Pocknee is inspired by, but not a mere repetition of Dearmer:

> It is necessary to recall that the ceremonial collection of alms at Matins and Evensong is a piece of Victorian 'ritualism' for which there is no authority in the Book of Common Prayer. Some incumbents, and even bishops, need to be reminded that at the reformation the Church of England did not institute the solemn elevation of the alms dish in the place of the late medieval ceremony of the elevation of the Host.

And there are areas in which he, like Dearmer, has been overtaken by events:

- The high altar of every church should have a canopy.
- Credence tables are a modern innovation.
- Evening Communion is a modern innovation.
- The chasuble should be removed before preaching.
- The stalls of the clergy should be returned and face east.
- The cap is usually worn in the open air.

The Parson's Handbook, like *Ritual Notes* and the Alcuin Club's *Directory of Ceremonial*, is now of largely historic interest; no one would want to use them to shape today's liturgy unless choosing to be deliberately and self-consciously antiquarian. One does not have to look very far for the main reason. The revised *Parson's Handbook* came a year after the Constitution on Sacred Liturgy of the Second Vatican Council. Pocknee anticipated further liturgical revision but he could not have expected such a radical disjunction. The liturgical upheaval removed old certainties and with them many of the concerns that fill the book. Pocknee's perspective was a broad one. He included, along with the details of liturgical use, such practical matters as the maintenance of the fabric of the building and the furnishings of vestries. But more importantly he stressed the need, in the face of liturgical fashion, for a degree of faithfulness to the tradition and an overall sense of dignity and order in worship, and all of these concerns remain relevant and important for the Church today.

SELECT BIBLIOGRAPHY

The Christian Altar in History and Today, Alcuin Club, 1963.
Cross and Crucifix in Christian Worship and Devotion, Alcuin Club, 1962.
The French Diocesan Hymns and Their Melodies, Alcuin Club Tract XXIX, 1954.
Liturgical Vesture: Its Origins and Development, Alcuin Club, 1960.
The Rites of Christian Initiation, Mowbray, 1962.
Revision of Percy Dearmer, *The Parson's Handbook*, 13th edn, Oxford University Press, 1965.

19

G. G. WILLIS

GORDON JEANES

It is through G. G. Willis that a generation of English-speaking scholars have learnt about the liturgy of the city of Rome.

Geoffrey Willis was born in Manchester on 6 July 1914, and read Latin at Manchester University. Ordained deacon in 1937 and priest in 1938, he served in the Diocese of Derby until 1958 and then was Vicar of Wing in Oxford until 1969, and for much of this time taught at Cuddesdon Theological College. From 1945 he served as a proctor in the Convocation of Canterbury, and in 1953 he was appointed Assistant Synodical Secretary and, in 1957, editor of the *Chronicle of the Convocation*. He retired from these posts in 1969, when he had lost his sight through diabetes. He carried on his academic work, relying on his memory and secretarial assistance, and his last work, a history of the Roman liturgy, was completed in the 1970s and published in 1994 along with a memoir of him by Michael Moreton. Willis died on 8 May 1982.

As we can see by this summary biography, Willis was involved in more than liturgy. In his scholarly work, he was known first for his work on St Augustine, publishing in 1950 *St Augustine and the Donatist Schism*. Later books, by W. H. C. Frend, Gerald Bonner, Peter Brown and many others, have pushed his contribution to the back of the library shelves, but it demonstrates none the less the careful detailed attention to the sources that is the hallmark of his liturgical work. In later years he was to attempt a reconstruction of St Augustine's lectionary from the preacher's sermons; this study arose from his work in the 1950s on the Convocation Joint Committee on the Lectionary.

His collections of *Essays* and *Further Essays in Early Roman Liturgy* were, and in many ways remain to this day, the most accessible appreciation of the development of the liturgy. These two volumes cover many details of the evolution of the Eucharist, but also other aspects of the worshipping life of the city: Ember Days, 'Mediana Week' (covering the fifth Sunday in Lent and the preceding Wednesday and Saturday), the Stational Liturgy, and the Consecration of Churches. Outside Rome he includes a study of the early English liturgy from Augustine to Alcuin. In the Eucharist he gives us histories of the variable prayers found in the sacramentaries, the intercessions and offertory prayers, the place of the Lord's Prayer, and the stylistic development of the canon in the relation of the various units within it to one another and the importance of the *cursus*, the rhythmical endings of the clauses which distinguished elegant Latin in the late Empire. It was for these volumes in particular that he was awarded a DD by the University of Nottingham in 1969.

There is something quintessentially English and Anglican in this approach to liturgy. There is little of theology; more of the learned footnote which seeks to follow up and explain the historical curiosities. And in the way in which he discusses the details of the liturgical text and introduces the reader to Continental studies, Willis presumes our fluency in Latin and Greek and our ignorance of contemporary languages.

But the learned footnote is something underestimated. Directly theological it may not be, but Willis's work is important in bringing home to the reader the various cultural influences. 'The Solemn Prayers of Good Friday' offers us a complete history of the intercessions of the early Roman rite, and a critical text (but not a translation) of the Solemn Prayers and of the later litany, the *Deprecatio S. Gelasii*, both of which had disappeared from frequent use in the early seventh century. Even today these texts deserve to be better known, as an example of liturgical intercession presenting a vision of a Christian society. (One detail of Willis's work has been corrected by later research: the *kyries* towards the beginning of the Mass are not the litany transferred to that position and reduced in length but are the remains of a separate litany taken from a stational procession. See J. Baldovin, 'Kyrie Eleison and the Entrance Rite of the Roman Eucharist', *Worship* 61, 1987.) And his study of the way in which the ancient intercessions were to be preserved only in the Good Friday liturgy is perhaps the most outstanding example of Baumstark's law that 'primitive conditions are maintained with greater tenacity in the more sacred seasons of the Liturgical Year'. His description of 'Roman Stational Liturgy', in which the choice of particular churches and processions to them involved all sections of the city and even the very streets of Rome in the worship of God, has paved the way for later studies into the urban character of early Christian worship, and gives material for us to reflect on the ritual relation between the gospel and society. Is Christian worship something which happens behind closed doors, or does it not embrace the community?

Willis's research coloured his own approach to contemporary liturgical revision. He was appointed a member of the new Church of England Liturgical Commission in 1955 and became its secretary. However, his membership of it was not always happy, and he resigned in 1965. Inevitably such a situation leads to a negative portrayal. But as we follow through his criticisms of Series 2 in *1966 and All That* and compare them with his academic work, we can see something of his more positive vision for liturgical reform.

Disliking the Eucharist of 1662 except insofar as it made tolerable that of 1552, Willis was attracted by the liturgy which he had studied in such depth. His final plea in this brief work for an acceptable eucharistic prayer – acceptable to very few indeed in the Church of England – was 'the Gregorian Canon in the superb English translation of Miles Coverdale'. And the two aspects of this proposal were equally dear to him. The Gregorian Canon represented the full flowering of the Roman liturgical tradition, and Miles Coverdale embodied a prose style which it is hard for this age to emulate, but which the Commission had rejected in its search for a contemporary style.

Willis's research does not show much interest in the beginnings of the Christian community in Rome. In the index of his *Essays*, Pope Leo the Great has more entries than Justin Martyr and Hippolytus combined, and Leo is easily bettered by Gregory. And it is the mature liturgy that Willis invoked as his model. Theologically he took Rome as his guide. Like some others on the Commission, he had hoped for a more explicit description of eucharistic offering in the Series 2 eucharistic prayer. When discussing the petition for consecration in *1966 and All That* he seems torn between the 1662 form – that those receiving the bread and wine may be partakers of the Body and Blood of Christ (an explicitly receptionist approach) – and the form to be found in the Roman Canon, that the bread and wine may become the Body and Blood of Christ. The Series 2 compromise, based on 1549, that they 'may be unto us' the Body and Blood of Christ, was somehow unacceptable. Compromise and ecclesiastical politics were not to his taste, but compromise and politics are ever the business of liturgical authorization.

The Roman rite of Gregory the Great was also for Willis the arbiter for the position of the Lord's Prayer, whether it followed the eucharistic prayer immediately or was a prelude to communion. And he opposed the idea of introducing the epiclesis of the Holy Spirit into any Western petition for consecration, seeing it as a later insertion in Hippolytus and a result of later Eastern developments of the Eucharist. (He was also opposed to the insertion of the epiclesis in modern Roman Catholic eucharistic prayers.)

The mention of Miles Coverdale makes Willis a natural ally of those who find the new liturgical style inadequate. Willis's preference was for the language of the Prayer Book, and therefore for Series 1 rather than Series 2, and he was impatient with attempts to devise a modern style of language for worship. It is perhaps in this respect more than in questions of theology that he questioned 'whether the wisest policy is to follow so early an authority as Hippolytus'. He was right to point out the awkwardness of trying to combine the full description of the works of God in creation and salvation as found in Hippolytus with the proper preface of the Roman rite and 1662, a system which still leads to repetition and a somewhat dislocated narrative. And against the style of Series 2, which he said 'has a tendency to be modern and ungraceful', he offered his own preference for the *cursus* as the key to good spoken prose in English as in Latin. Here we have very much the researcher and the reviser of liturgy as one and the same person, and no doubt we also have the reason for the careful but laboured defence by Commission members of the language of the modern liturgy in its use of the *cursus* and other classical rhetorical forms, for example in R. C. D. Jasper's *The Eucharist Today* (London, SPCK, 1974).

There is an extra irony in Willis's rejection of the Series 2 intercessions. ('Its structure is formless and confused; its language is pedestrian and inaccurate, and it is quite unusable.') According to Ronald Jasper, their structure was based on the Roman Solemn Prayers for Good Friday which Willis himself had caused to be so well known.

Such is the picture given to us by *1966 and All That*. It raises the question whether Willis's work belongs to some other age than that of the 1960s. Theologically, his reliance on all things Roman, and his ignoring the reality of liturgical revision in a post-Reformation Church of England, might seem to ally him with an earlier generation of Anglo-Catholics. In the question of language and the role of liturgy in Church and society, much of what he has to offer might be more appropriate today than thirty years ago. Then, it was becoming increasingly difficult to maintain the ideal of seventeenth-century language, and a twentieth-century language for worship had to be invented. It was not going to spring forth fully grown like Athene from Zeus's head. Willis's studies had little to offer at that time, for by temperament he wished to work with the traditional rather than invent the new. But now when we look again at how a form of worship matures and integrates with the culture, embracing it with the gospel of Christ, then perhaps Willis has still much to teach us.

SELECT BIBLIOGRAPHY

Essays in Early Roman Liturgy, Alcuin Club Collections XLVI, SPCK, 1964.

Further Essays in Early Roman Liturgy, Alcuin Club Collections L, SPCK, 1964.

A History of the Early Roman Liturgy, with a memoir of the author by Michael Moreton, Henry Bradshaw Society Subsidia, no. 1, Boydell Press, 1994.

'Sacrificium Laudis', in B. D. Spinks (ed.), *The Sacrifice of Praise*, Ephemerides Liturgical Subsidia (Centro Liturgico Vincenziano, Rome) 1981, pp. 73–87.

St Augustine and the Donatist Controversy, SPCK, 1950.

St Augustine's Lectionary, Alcuin Club Collections XLIV, SPCK, 1962.

1966 and All That: Revision of the Eucharist in the Church of England, League of Anglican Loyalists, 1969.

'The New Eucharistic Prayers: Some Comments', *Heythrop Journal* 12, 1971, pp. 5–28.

20

J. G. DAVIES

GORDON WAKEFIELD

There is a masterly article by Professor Daniel W. Hardy on 'God in the Ordinary: The Work of J. G. Davies (1919–1990)' in the November/December 1996 issue of the journal *Theology*. This reviews Davies' achievement in the Department of Theology at the University of Birmingham, where he worked for forty years, and traces his theological development from his first book on *The Theology of William Blake* (1948) via his Bampton lectures of 1958, *He Ascended into Heaven*, to his counterblast to Rudolf Otto, *Everyday God: Encountering the Holy in World and Worship* (1973). These and many more were accompanied from the beginning by essays on liturgy, reaching a climax with the editing of the *Dictionary of Liturgy and Worship* in 1972 and its successor of 1986. In some respects he went his own way and was not a member of the Church of England Liturgical Commission, though Hardy says that his chairmanship of a working group of the World Council of Churches on 'The Missionary Structure of the Congregation' was decisive in shaping the theology of his last twenty years. His work became less Church-centred after the WCC report, more devoted to the Church's participation in the mission of God-in-Christ to the world and fearful lest the Church became the prison house of the devout. For many years he never practised as a priest or wore clerical dress. He was affected by the secular theology of the 1960s, yet his writings are convincingly Christian and incarnational. I recall him saying at the first Departmental meeting I attended that he believed that Jesus really lived, and Hardy records his frequent declaration

'I am a fourth-century Trinitarian'. He was Chalcedonian in Christology and basic to his understanding of liturgy was his belief that in Christ the two natures, divine and human, were united. This underlay his conviction that there should be no dichotomy between the sacred and the secular.

By any standards, his was an outstanding mind which united technical skill, an immense range of knowledge and an interest in practicalities from politics to pilgrimage, with an especial expertise in architecture, sculpture and the arts far beyond the bounds of his own country.

We may consider first his liturgical interest in architecture. In 1952, he wrote on *Early Christian Church Architecture*, a finely illustrated production with some account of the immense variety of plans due in large part to geographical distribution. He investigates the origin of the basilica and its different types, examines the central type of architecture with its round, octagonal and cruciform plans, describes church furnishings and appointments and gives a brief, generalized account of the forms Christian architecture assumed in different countries. In his book of 1979 *From Temple to Meeting House: The Phenomenology and Theology of Places of Worship*, Harold W. Turner refers frequently to Davies, always with approval of his scholarship, not least of the 1952 book. Davies had gone on to found, with Gilbert Cope, the Birmingham Institute for Worship and Religious Architecture, written *The Architectural Setting of Baptism* and helped to design the Highgate Baptist Church and the Church of SS Philip and James, Hodge Hill, both in Birmingham. He believed that buildings should be designed in accordance with the liturgy and co-operated in *An Experimental Liturgy* of the Diocese of Birmingham. Gordon Davies called it an 'Aunt Sally to stimulate discussion of the form that a revised liturgy might take'.

In his work on architecture and theology, he was well aware of the way in which buildings expressed spirituality. In an article on the subject in *The Expository Times* (1962) he wrote of Gothic forms which, both inside and outside, rise from earth to heaven, whereas a 'Byzantine building . . . is essentially 'hanging architecture'; its vaults drip from above without any weight of their own; the columns are not supports but descending tentacles; the whole develops downwards in accordance with the hierarchical spirituality manifest throughout Byzantine life'. He himself came to deplore the belief that church buildings should be expressions of the numinous in a profane world. This might be true of the Old Testament, but was incompatible with belief in the Incarnation. In 1968 he wrote on *The Secular Use of Church Buildings*, an historical study, which lamented the increasing division between sacred and secular as social activities were removed from the naves of churches. In his brief commendatory foreword to Patrick Cowley's Alcuin Club book *The Church House*, he asserts that the dichotomy between the sacred and the secular is

> contrary to the teaching of Jesus and is flatly denied by the sacramental principle at least as it is accepted in the Church of England . . . Christians, who are men and women 'in Christ', bear less than a true witness to their Lord if their practice in relation to church buildings separates the material and the spiritual, the sacred and the secular.

This is contrary to the instinctive feelings of many of the faithful. The penultimate chapter of *The Secular Use of Church Buildings*, 'The Problem of Church-building', approaches the subject from consideration of the nature of God and the function of the Christian community in the world. Is the God for whom churches are to be erected 'one who delights in monuments to his honour rather than in loving care for men? A church building may be the expression of devotion to a false, even tribal God, who is less humane than many of his creatures.' We have not so learnt Christ, in whose ministry the prominent works 'are not those of sanctification and sacrifice, but works of healing and proclamation, invitation and instruction, service and calling'.

There is a discussion of the nature of the Kingdom of God, the Divine rule, 'righteousness and *shalom* and joy in the Holy Spirit'. Its object is the salvation of the world, which must always have priority. The servant Church should provide multi-purpose buildings for the service of humanity. There is a lengthy critique of the belief that there are two worlds, the sacred and the profane, and that the latter must be abandoned to enter the former. This attitude has dominated Christianity from the fourth century at the latest. Entrance into the realm of the divine, the sanctuary, must be carefully regulated, and among extremists to this day, laity are not to enter beyond the screen, except for communion, and certainly not pass beyond the altar rails, and women may not so much as carry flowers to the altar. This Davies demolishes, with a critique of Otto on the way, as entirely alien to the New Testament. We may in fact isolate God and put up barriers against him, shut him in, rather than the secular out. Davies insists that the multi-purpose building must not screen off the sanctuary from the part used for other activities, as has happened so often since the Second World War. This completely defeats the object of uniting sacred and secular.

Davies's liturgical convictions may be summarized as participation and creativity. They are encapsulated in *New Perspectives on Worship Today* (1978). As ever, the work is redolent of scholarship as he analyses Play, Dance, Sexuality, Conflict, Politics and Laughter as having place in worship. He is against the constant devising and revising of liturgies by expert commissions. They should emerge from the people. 'Worship begins with human beings and not with books, not even with prayer books.' A congregation is not an audience, as in a theatre or at a concert. He does not share the view that there may be intense participation through simply listening passively and being caught up into heaven. The ordained minister may find his liturgical role by looking for 'the locked up creativity in others in order somehow to release it'. Davies is aware that his new perspectives involve risk, but 'Christ summons us not to security, to dull routine, to repetitive prayers, to worship by rote'.

A special concern is treated in detail in *Liturgical Dance: An Historical, Theological, and Practical Handbook*. The bibliography is vast. He treats religious dance as a universal phenomenon, but finds in Christianity an ambivalence towards it. There always have been those fearful of eroticism, degradation and paganism, though in the West it was widely practised in churches. Much Protestantism tended to condemn it, though one must not generalize. There is now 'a burgeoning of religious dance the like of which has not been seen in Christianity before'. Davies wants to give this a theological rationale, which he does by rejecting the age-old division of body and soul as contrary to original Christian understanding and maintaining that for Christians God is a God of movement 'in whom we live and move and have our being'. Movement as well as words may praise him.

Dance often has an erotic quality which leads Davies to reproduce passages on Sexuality from *New Perspectives*. Eroticism is the affirmation of life. It may be lust, but dance may control it through a ritualized form. A very fine discussion of sacraments leads to the conclusion that dance is a 'sacramental', an act which accompanies and interprets the sacraments or a part of them. It also increases the joy in God and his acts which the sacraments express and their cohesive and corporate nature. Liturgical dance may sometimes be mourning as well as joy. 'It emanates from the interior drive of the dancers as they give honour to their Lord; and it is appropriate to the divine mystery before which babble should from time to time be suppressed in favour of a voiceless but bodily communion.'

When he turns to practicalities, Davies considers movement prayer. If we mean what we say in our prayers and are earnest in our praise, penitence and desires, we should not be motionless in our bodies. He supplies 'A Christian Vocabulary of Bodily Parts, Posture and Movement'. He shows how the Lord's Prayer may be movement-prayer. All this demands much preparation in the congregation, as indeed does liturgical dance by a group of trained dancers who will act as representatives of the people as a whole with whom the non-dancers can identify. Davies goes on to show how dance may enable the deaf to share more fully in worship and save the handicapped from feeling isolated as movements are designed for them. He looks for a time when congregations may dance regularly in honour of God, thus rejecting a docetism 'which denies the very nature with which

God has both endowed its members and has glorified through his Son'.

In the year *Liturgical Dance* was published, Gordon Davies with P. van Zyl and F. M. Young reconstructed a Shaker Dance Liturgy. This was one of the last productions of the Institute of Worship and Religious Architecture before it was wound up. Its prescriptions for worship were 'Sing a little, dance a little, exhort a little, preach a little, and a good many littles will make a great deal'. The prayer is extempore, but the dances and marches are very much in formation, spontaneous, or out of step.

Davies was a prophetic voice in liturgy. His prophecies have been half-fulfilled; church buildings have more secular use; dance has burgeoned in some places, usually by trained dance choirs. Participation is a *sine qua non*. Davies does not sufficiently recognize that for Methodists it has been achieved by hymn singing. At Hodge Hill, the sanctuary in the midst of secular ancillaries and tennis in the 'congregational space', did not make Christians. The attempt to have a 'joke session' in worship stumbled on the threshold of the risqué.

Davies aroused opposition among ordinary churchgoers, which is not to say that he was wrong in principle. As a liturgist, he leaves a remarkable example of immense scholarship, an awareness of the necessity of history and not simply in the main traditions, and, above all, the need for liturgy to be the expression of Christian theology.

SELECT BIBLIOGRAPHY

The Architectural Setting of Baptism, Barrie and Rockliffe, 1962.

Editor with fifty-four entries, *A Dictionary of Liturgy and Worship*, SCM Press, 1972.

Editor with seventy-five entries, *A New Dictionary of Liturgy and Worship*, SCM Press, 1986.

Everyday God: Encountering the Holy in World and Worship, SCM Press, 1973.

Holy Week: A Short History, Lutterworth Press, 1963.

Life and Worship in the Early Church, SCM Press, 1954.

Liturgical Dance: An Historical, Theological and Practical Handbook, SCM Press, 1984.
New Perspectives in Worship Today, SCM Press, 1978.
The Origin and Development of Early Christian Church Architecture, SCM Press, 1952.
The Secular Use of Church Buildings, SCM Press, 1968.
A Select Liturgical Lexicon, Lutterworth Press, 1965.
The Spirit, the Church and the Sacraments, Faith Press, 1954.
Temples, Churches and Mosques: A Guide to the Appreciation of Religious Architecture, Blackwell, 1982.
Worship and Mission, SCM Press, 1966.

21

E. C. WHITAKER

DONALD GRAY

It is to be hoped that no variation in patterns of ministry, nor modification in our manner of training the clergy, nor any other ecclesiastical, sociological or academic change, will contribute to the extermination of a unique Anglican phenomenon – the scholar parson. In the field of liturgy no one, in recent years, has fulfilled that role with more shy dignity, coupled with immense erudition, than Edward Charles Whitaker, who served for forty years as a parish priest in Cumbria, seventeen years as Vicar of Kirby Ireleth, followed by eight years as Vicar of Plumpton Wall in the Diocese of Carlisle.

It was to a remote country parish in Kirby-in-Furness that in 1965 the summons came for its Vicar to join the Liturgical Commission of the Church of England. He joined it at a particularly crucial time. Ronald Jasper had just taken over from Donald Coggan as Chairman and the Series 2 proposals were about to be published and submitted to the Convocations and the Church Assembly. During the next fifteen years the influence of Charles Whitaker was of the greatest significance in the Commission's output, despite the fact that few outside the circle of liturgical scholars (and not all of them) would have known his name. Certainly, bishops, Assembly and Synod members and the various church officials would have passed him in the corridors of Church House without a flicker of recognition. Though it must be admitted that his visits to Westminster were as infrequent as he could decently arrange.

STUDENT OF CHRISTIAN INITIATION

The question remains: why was Whitaker plucked out of obscurity, when there was certainly no lack of candidates among the clergy of England, anxious to put the liturgy right? In a tiny autobiographical section in a booklet he produced in 1960, he momentarily lifted the curtain. In that he described himself as 'a student who has spent years studying the baptismal rites of both the Eastern and the Western Church in such spare time as parochial duties allow, and believes he has a fairly competent knowledge of their meaning and history'. Earlier that year he had given evidence of the 'competent knowledge' with the publication of *Documents of the Baptismal History.* This is a book which will long remain an essential tool in the hands of those who would study Christian Initiation. It contains translations of the texts of baptismal rites, where they exist, along with descriptions *inter alia* of such ceremonies. It commences with the Ante-Nicene Church and ends with the Sarum Rite. It is a mine of liturgical information.

Having demonstrated his wide knowledge of the basic baptismal texts, Whitaker believed that it would not be improper for him to comment on the services of baptism and confirmation which had recently been produced. The early days of the Commission had been dogged by internal arguments over baptismal services. Just before the setting up of the Liturgical Commission the York Convocation had drawn up its own service, and Eric Milner-White and Eric Evans, both from the northern province, and both members of the Commission, actively promoted the York Rite over against the Commission's own proposals. When the Commission presented a report in 1958 they insisted on appending a dissenting note. Whitaker had no time for the York service. 'Its progenitors', he wrote, 'seem happy in the dubious distinction of having framed the only baptismal rite in Christendom which has no pattern.' In this he echoed the attack which had been made on the service in the journal *Theology* by E. C. Ratcliff. He caustically commented 'It would be interesting to know in what respects the historic liturgies may be supposed to have contributed materially to the making of York. Their traces have been well concealed.'

Whitaker believed, however, that the 1958 report had produced something 'worthy to hold a place among the other classical manifestations of the Church's liturgy'. This is a quotation from a booklet Whitaker produced for SPCK in which he made sympathetic, though not uncritical examination, of the Commission's 1958 proposals. Acknowledging the fact that he had spent years studying historic initiation rites, none the less he insisted that he was judging them as a pastor. 'As a priest whose ministry has been spent exclusively in parochial work . . . the judgement of the pastor ought to be final in this matter. No rite, however technically perfect, can be of any real use to the Church if it does not satisfy her pastoral needs.'

THE WORK OF THE COMMISSION

It was in that spirit that he joined the Commission in 1965. It may well be that his lifelong friendship with Bernard Wigan, who was one of the Commission's original members, had been influential in bringing his name to the attention of the archbishops, but he quickly proved to be the right man in the right place, however surprised he may personally have been now to find himself involved in the inner councils of the Church. Over the next few years he not only played a significant part in the Commission's deliberations around the meeting table, but was a hard-working and diligent draftsman of a variety of services, not just baptism and confirmation. He had the ability to write simply and clearly not only in the drafting of services, but in the commentaries which were needed to introduce and explain the new services to a wider, and often sceptical, public. Whitaker was an accomplished apologist for liturgical revision, but he preferred the written word to platform appearances, and even then he continued to be at pains to emphasize that he wrote primarily as a parish priest – and not as a scholar.

By 1965 it was recognized that it was becoming increasingly urgent that there should be a series of baptism and confirmation services on the table. The bishops were pressing, in particular, for the early introduction of what they chose to describe as a new 'simple' service of Infant Baptism. The majority of the Commission were of the opinion that the earlier proposals were on the right lines, but Jasper noted that 'It was now a great help to have Charles Whitaker's expert knowledge on the subject, which he contrived to offer with considerable patience and modesty.' In the event the proposals, although very little changed from the 1958 report, secured a quick and easy passage through the legislative process, and all was well, for a while.

In terms of painstaking and detailed work there is nothing more tedious and potentially boring than work on calendar and lectionary, to say nothing of the compilation of the inevitable consequence: 'Rule to Order the Service'. Undaunted, Charles Whitaker undertook this thankless task. His commitment to the enterprise earned him the distinction of being the subject of one of the few liturgical jokes that came out of that period of otherwise serious endeavour. Jasper tells the story in full detail:

> It was a complicated and tedious business, involving constant checking and cross-checking and requiring capacity to carry an immense amount of detail in the mind. Fortunately the ideal person to do all this was available in Charles Whitaker, who had the necessary patience and diligence; although regarded as the Commission's expert on Initiation matters, he shouldered this additional burden without demur; and it was with reason that the Commission regarded the resulting report as 'Whitaker's Almanac'.

The Church of England has for years had a long-running debate around the whole subject of Initiation, including discussions about the theological propriety of the baptism of infants; the right age for confirmation (even the questioning of the necessity of this rite at all); the admission of children for communion. The timetable for the final stages of the ASB was threatened by the rerunning of these debates, fuelled by the Ely Report, which proposed that baptism be recognized as the full and complete rite of Christian initiation. Eventually proposals, which are the basis of the ASB services, were drafted and they included, of course, more careful work undertaken by Whitaker.

They were rites which did not take sides on the issue of whether initiation is complete in water baptism or needs in some way to be 'completed' in the post-baptismal ceremony of Confirmation. Whitaker himself commented, 'Since Synod reached no theological conclusion and declined to make any considerable change in pastoral practice, it was left to the Liturgical Commission to draft rites of baptism and confirmation which observed a theological neutrality, not favouring either point of view to the exclusion of the other.'

In his last published writing he provided not only a theological critique of the resulting ASB service, but an invaluable practical guide to the ordered performance of the rites. It is once again – and finally – the work of the parson scholar, anxious that there should be no dichotomy between liturgical and theological exactitude and dignified and correctly conducted services. This was typically the work of a distinguished scholar and priest who in one of his parishes acted as postman. In those days the post still came on Christmas Day, and so it was his delight both to take the services in Church and to deliver the cards and parcels around the parish, providing him with an opportunity of wishing everyone personally a very happy Christmas. The Anglican scholar parson: a rare breed indeed; may it never die out.

SELECT BIBLIOGRAPHY

The Baptismal Liturgy, SPCK, 1981. (Originally published as Studies in Christian Worship V, Faith Press, 1965.)

Documents of the Baptismal Liturgy, 2nd edn, 1970. (Originally published as Alcuin Club Collections XLII, 1960.)

The Intercessions of the Prayer Book, SPCK, 1956.

Martin Bucer and the Book of Common Prayer, Alcuin Club Collections LV, 1974.

The New Services – a guide and explanation, SPCK, 1967.

The Proposed Services of Baptism and Confirmation Considered, SPCK, 1967.

22

G. J. CUMING

DONALD GRAY

Each period of Anglican liturgical study seems to need its mentor. There is no doubt that liturgy is the 'Cinderella' subject of most theological faculties and departments. Even the most distinguished professor of theology is capable of recycling Dean Inge's put-down in which he is alleged to have expressed as little interest in liturgy as in philately. Consequently liturgy needs its heroes, those whose scholarship and academic excellence cannot be faulted even by those who have nothing but disdain for the speciality.

Between about 1970 and his too early death in 1988, Geoffrey Cuming fulfilled that role in England – and increasingly across the Anglican Communion.

A son of the Vicarage, he was educated at Eton and served both in bomb disposal and in the Parachute Field Ambulance during the 1939–45 War. He was injured at Arnhem and invalided out of the Army just before the end of the war. As a result of his wartime injuries he suffered lasting and continuous pain for the rest of his life.

HISTORIAN OF THE PRAYER BOOK

A graduate of Oriel, the college associated with many of the original Tractarians, he trained for the priesthood at Westcott House, Cambridge, and left there to work in the diocese of Blackburn, serving his title in an urban parish – St Stephen's Burnley. However, he had already been marked out for his academic ability and in 1950 he was invited to join the staff of

St John's College Durham as a tutor, sharing the task of training ordinands in what was a boom period for Anglican theological colleges. He became Vice-Principal of St John's, and it was while in Durham that he first became interested in the history of The Book of Common Prayer and took his first step in establishing himself as a historian of Anglican liturgy.

At the Restoration of the Monarchy in 1660 there had been an attempt by the two most prominently surviving followers of Archbishop Laud (John Cosin and Matthew Wren) to restore the characteristic elements of the more 'High Church' 1549 Prayer Book. It was hoped to do that, if possible, without alienating a House of Commons who would have been quite content to revive the more 'Protestant' book of 1604. This task was then further complicated by an attempt to reconcile the Presbyterians to using the Prayer Book at all. They asked that either a new liturgy be compiled, 'or at least to revise and effectively reform the old'. The King, wanting to preserve the peace, promised to appoint 'learned divines of different persuasions to review the Book of Common Prayer'. At some time during the winter of 1660–61, John Cosin began to enter the various suggestions for revision in a folio Prayer Book of 1619. This is known as 'the Durham Book' and is preserved in the Cosin Library in the University of Durham. This had never been satisfactorily transcribed – and was a task awaiting a suitably dedicated and qualified scholar. The book is obviously of significant importance in the history of the liturgy of the Church of England. Cuming started on this major piece of historical and liturgical research, not realizing where it would eventually lead him.

His work on the Durham Book continued when he left St John's to become Vicar of Billesdon in the diocese of Leicester in 1955. The Principal of St John's (R. R. Williams) had become Bishop of Leicester and had invited Cuming to join him. Later, in 1963, Bishop Williams moved him to the suburban parish of Humberstone. The meticulous edition of the Durham Book was published in 1961 and he was awarded the degree of Doctor of Divinity by the University of Oxford. Already he had embarked upon a further project in Prayer Book history. For many years theological students, and others, had relied upon a history of the Prayer Book and its sources known as Procter and Frere. It had its origins in a book written in the middle of the nineteenth century by Francis Procter and revised by W. H. Frere in 1900. Cuming decided that, rather than another rejuvenation, he would tackle an entirely new work. This definitive work first appeared in 1967, but by 1982 there had been such a flurry of liturgical activity that a second edition was needed. The new edition brought the story up to date, and by now Geoffrey Cuming had an important part in that history.

HIS INFLUENCE ON THE ASB

Ronald Jasper knew of Cuming's work, and although they had never met, he was keen that the Liturgical Commission should have the knowledge and expertise of this scholar with his knowledge of the history and development of the liturgy in the Church of England. He became a member in 1965 and remained on the Commission until the publication of the Alternative Service Book (ASB) in 1980. He became Jasper's right-hand man, particularly in the final five years of work on the new book. In his book *The Development of the Anglican Liturgy* Jasper describes in detail the work of bringing to birth the ASB. He pays grateful tribute to the work of Cuming at various stages of the process, for instance, his drafting of the first 'you' texts and his work on the funeral and ordination rites. However, Jasper particularly acknowledges the work Cuming did in adapting each of these services, which had already been given approval by Synod, so that there was uniformity throughout the book. Then, that having been achieved, there was the monumental task of editing. Jasper said that he was 'invaluable in the thankless task of cross-checking'. Cuming served as Vice-Chairman of the Commission, but in one aspect that was not an onerous task – the Chairman was never absent. Despite that, he was very much needed as a source of sound wisdom and discreet advice to Jasper. He described him as 'a genial giant'. Certainly his contribution to the ASB in many varied ways was immense.

PATRISTIC SCHOLAR

Although all Cuming's published writings for nearly sixty years were associated with the history of Anglican worship, from 1974 onwards he made many distinguished contributions to the wider field of liturgical scholarship and moved into Patristic studies.

In 1975 he translated and edited, with Ronald Jasper, a set of texts which has become a standard work for students of liturgy. Entitled *Prayers of the Eucharist, Early and Reformed*, it was three times revised and expanded. The next year he published the first of a number of works on the *Apostolic Tradition* of Hippolytus. By this time he had been teaching liturgy for a number of years at King's College, London, in succession to Ronald Jasper, and he had discovered that Dom Gregory Dix's 1938 edition of Hippolytus, although indispensable to scholars, was 'never really suitable for beginners, who were bewildered by the very fullness of the textual apparatus'. In 1978 he edited a series of essays by Charles Whitaker and Paul Bradshaw and himself on various aspects of the work of Hippolytus. There then followed articles on Serapion, the Liturgy of St James and finally, and posthumously, he crowned an increasing interest in Egyptian liturgy with a definitive edition of liturgy of the patriarchate of Alexandria, known as the Liturgy of St Mark.

Cuming was also interested in the search for the most ancient form of the eucharistic prayer, believing that those involved in composing modern eucharistic prayers might usefully look further back than the fourth-century anaphoras which they usually took as their model. The result would be, he believed, a more concise rite which would contain less duplication and would be, at one and the same time, both primitive and contemporary.

This work in the Patristic era earned him the respect of liturgical scholars throughout the world and he was a valued and welcome contributor to international and ecumenical seminars and symposia, particularly the Congress of Societas Liturgica and at the Oxford Patristic Conferences. For a number of years he edited the papers of the Ecclesiastical History Society in its *Studies in Church History* series.

Cuming moved from King's College, London, to teach at Cuddesdon College (later Ripon College Cuddesdon), Oxford, in 1974. From 1981 he regularly taught and lectured at American universities. It was while in Texas in 1988 that he died suddenly, when seemingly recovering well from a surgical operation. Together with his teaching on both sides of the Atlantic, he found a particular vocation in the encouragement of younger scholars. In 1978 he suggested the setting up of a permanent forum for younger liturgical scholars in Britain and this led to the formation of the Society for Liturgical Study. They naturally made him their first President.

In the last two decades of his life Geoffrey was instrumental in restoring the international reputation of Anglican liturgical scholarship and furthermore left behind him a small but devoted band of disciples who, inspired by his example of what Henry Chadwick called 'an unerring eye for precise detail', hopefully will carry the torch into the twenty-first century.

SELECT BIBLIOGRAPHY

The Durham Book, Oxford University Press, 1961.
(ed. with R. C. D. Jasper) *Prayers of the Eucharist, Early and Reformed*, Collins, 1975; Pueblo, 1987.
Hippolytus: A Text for Students, Grove Liturgical Study 8, 1976.
A History of Anglican Liturgy, Macmillan, 2nd edn, 1981.
The Godly Order, Alcuin Club Collections LXV, 1983.
The Liturgy of St James, Orientalia Christiana Analecta 234, Rome, 1990.

23

R. C. D. JASPER

DONALD GRAY

In the aftermath of both the twentieth-century World Wars the Church of England gave itself to a period of frenetic liturgical activity. In 1904 the Royal Commission on Ecclesiastical Discipline had firmly stated as their opinion that 'the law of public worship in the Church of England is too narrow for the religious life of the present generation'. The Royal Commission recommended that Letters of Business be given to the Convocations which would enable them to produce revised services more suited to Church folk of the new century.

Despite working through the Great War only slow progress was made. This wartime activity offered some critics the opportunity to make wry comments on the Church's priorities. While thousands were being killed, with or without the ministrations of the Church, they commented, the Church's Convocations were occupied with the minutiae of liturgical revision. Yet at the same time there was a good deal of evidence that the unbending provisions of the Book of Common Prayer were being tried, tested and found considerably wanting in the trenches of Flanders and Gallipoli.

The history of the failure of the 1927 and 1928 revisions has still to be fully detailed and assessed, but it had the result that by the Second World War the Church of England still had unfinished liturgical business. It was almost eighty years after the recommendations of the Royal Commission that authorized alternatives to the Book of Common Prayer were finally provided.

PREPARING THE GROUND

One man gave almost his entire working life to bringing about this long-awaited objective. Ronald Claud Dudley Jasper was appointed to the Liturgical Commission on its foundation in 1955. This was something of a surprise to him – and other members of the Commission. He was not then widely known as a liturgical scholar, and he took his place at the table alongside such luminaries as E. C. Ratcliff, Eric Milner-White and Geoffrey Willis. The reason he was there was that he had been talent-spotted some years before by Bishop Colin Dunlop, whom the archbishop had selected to chair the Commission. Dunlop, as Bishop of Jarrow, had come to know Jasper when he was curate of St Oswald's, Durham. Between 1823 and 1876 the Vicar of St Oswald's had been John Bacchus Dyke, one of those involved in the production of *Hymns Ancient and Modern* – an often underestimated seminal point in the liturgical development within the Church of England.

Until the publication of 'A & M', hymn singing had been widely outlawed by the High-Churchmen. Discovering about the furore that had been caused by this and other of Dyke's innovations awakened an interest in the young historian (he had already obtained his Master's degree in history). Eventually the results of his researches were published in 1954 as *Prayer Book Revision in England 1800–1900.*

In the same year Jasper completed another major piece of work in the field of liturgical history, which took the story of the Church of England's struggle to discover a modern liturgical identity a little further into the twentieth century. Jasper had read history at Leeds University and trained for the priesthood at the College of the Resurrection, Mirfield. Although never taught there by Walter Frere, Jasper, who was born in Plymouth in 1917, met him in the south-west while Frere was Bishop of Truro. Colin Dunlop suggested Jasper might edit Frere's liturgical papers, and the Alcuin Club published them as their Collection for 1954. This work gave Jasper an insight, for instance, into the tensions and problems experienced between 1912 and 1916 by the Advisory Committee on Liturgical

Questions. This was the committee of liturgical experts, working on what became the 1927/28 proposals, which most nearly approximates to the Liturgical Commission set up in 1955. Jasper later used this knowledge to warn the archbishops of potential pitfalls – some of which were not avoided, he believed.

THE LITURGICAL COMMISSION

The work of the Commission was at first slow and unadventurous. The average age of the commissioners was high; a third had been born in the nineteenth century. A combination of caution on the part of the Chairman, together with a low level of enthusiasm emanating from both Lambeth and Bishopthorpe, guaranteed that little of great interest was produced in its first years. After a loosening of the 'rules of management' under the chairmanship of Bishop (later Archbishop) Donald Coggan, there was then a significant leap forward after Ronald Jasper took over the chair in 1964.

It was not that the needs of those many parishes which had been influenced by the Parish Communion Movement began to be considered. The Parish Communion had its origins in the liturgical enthusiasms of the Christian Socialists in the latter part of the nineteenth century. One of the earliest examples was Walter Frere's introduction of a 9.30 a.m. Parish Communion at St Faith's, Stepney in 1892. Between the wars, inspired by the writing of Gabriel Hebert, and after 1948, following the formation of the Parish and People Movement, the introduction of a simply sung Communion Service – held between 9 and 10 a.m. with the congregation communicating and often followed by a Parish Breakfast – was rapid and widespread.

Jasper, who had himself introduced a Parish Communion as priest-in-charge of St Giles, Durham, and subsequently built parish life at Stillington – where he was incumbent from 1948 to 1955 – around such a service, was sensitive to both the pastoral as well as the liturgical needs of such congregations. In the crucial years during which the contents of The Alternative Service Book (ASB) were being put together the Church of England was fortunate to have as the chairman of its Liturgical

Commission a scholar who had spent fifteen years as a parish priest in industrial England and who was well aware of the contemporary situation in the average parish.

ECUMENICAL LITURGICAL CO-OPERATION

Ronald Jasper was equally sensitive to a further important development in the life of the Church. This has been called 'The Ecumenical Century', but until the 1960s the fact that the Liturgical Movement had begun to influence each of the major denominations had been little acknowledged across the denominations by any practical co-operation among their scholars. The Faith and Order movement had prepared a factual report, *Ways of Worship*, back in 1951, yet each church was still busy with its own changes and revisions with little or no regard or interest in what their Christian neighbours were about.

When Jasper moved in 1960 from being Succentor of Exeter Cathedral to a lectureship at King's College, London, he came into contact with clergy and scholars from other traditions who had similar liturgical interests. He was initially inspired by a paper given by Dr John Lamb of the Church of Scotland. Jasper said that he realized that talking about liturgy was not enough: creating liturgy together would be more productive and offer more opportunity for progress towards Christian unity than any other approach. It was to be a highly significant realization, which was to lead him into hitherto uncharted waters.

The Joint Liturgical Group (JLG), comprising representatives from all the major denominations in Great Britain, was formed in 1963 with Jasper as its Secretary and diligent facilitator. He edited the Group's influential reports on *Calendar and Lectionary*, *The Daily Office*, *Holy Week Services*, *Worship and Child* and others. Three years later, in 1966, he was invited to be one of the official ecumenical observers at the Consilium in Rome. This was the body which had been mandated to work out the practical consequences of the Constitution on the Liturgy, one of the earliest products of the Second Vatican Council summoned by Pope John XXIII in 1962. It was these contacts in

Rome, together with the now full participation of the Roman Catholic Church in the work of the JLG, that inspired the formation of the International Consultation on English Texts (ICET). This was the forum in which the English-speaking Church worldwide could come together in order to agree on modern translations of those liturgical texts which all had in common. The effect of this was that, although quite often churches have to worship separately, yet they could do so in the knowledge that they were using the same liturgical texts as their friends in other churches. The texts were published under the title *Prayers We Have in Common* and have been used in revised service books world, and denominationally, wide.

Ronald Jasper was also involved in the inauguration of Societas Liturgica – the international and ecumenical 'learned society' of liturgical scholars, and was President from 1969 to 1971. The Societas congresses gave him further opportunity to widen and deepen his ecumenical friendships in the field of liturgy as up to 200 liturgical scholars from all parts of the world, and from various traditions, came together to discuss liturgical matters of common interest.

In 1968 he became a Canon of Westminster. He remained at the Abbey until 1975, when he returned to the north of England to become Dean of York. During his first five years in York he bore the double burden of the Deanery and the Chairmanship of the Liturgical Commission at the most crucial stage in the production of the ASB, but he never neglected either of these important tasks. Sadly, his ministry at York came to a dramatic conclusion. During the night of 9 July 1984, and only days before his retirement, a lightning bolt struck the Minster and the roof of the south transept was destroyed. He retired to Ripon where he died on 11 April 1990.

ABIDING INFLUENCE

It can be stated with confidence that no one has had a greater influence on the course of Church of England liturgical revision in this century than Ronald Jasper. In fact, his eventual and daunting task was to oversee the greatest changes in the worship of the Church of England since 1662. He approached his work with the thoroughness of a trained historian. He never claimed to be a literary stylist, more than once firmly declaring that he was 'not another Cranmer'. Yet he wrestled with the problem of discovering a liturgical language for today. He was firmly of the opinion that such a voyage of discovery must of necessity be an ecumenical one. Hence his enthusiasm for both JLG and ICET. Of this work he wrote,

> Whatever future generations may say about us – we have tried – prayerfully and conscientiously – to do what we believe to have been right, to help men worship God in a worthier and more meaningful way. It has occupied some of us for something like twenty years of our lives. I for one would not have missed it for worlds.

SELECT BIBLIOGRAPHY

A Companion to the Alternative Service Book (with P. F. Bradshaw), SPCK, 1986.

The Development of Anglican Liturgy 1662–1980, SPCK, 1989.

Prayer Book Revision in England 1800–1900, SPCK, 1954.

Prayers of the Eucharist: Early and Reformed (with G. J. Cuming), 3rd enlarged edn, Pueblo, 1987.

The Search for an Apostolic Liturgy, Alcuin Club Pamphlet XVIII, Mowbray, 1963.

Walter Frere: his Correspondence on Liturgical Revision and Construction, Alcuin Club Collections XXXIX, SPCK, 1954.

INDEX

THE ALCUIN CLUB

The Alcuin Club exists to promote the study of Christian liturgy in general, and in particular the liturgies of the Anglican Communion. Since its foundation in 1897, it has published nearly 150 books, studies and pamphlets. Members of the Club receive some publications of the current year free and others at a reduced price.

The Club works in partnership with GROW in the publication of its Joint Liturgical Studies series, is one of the sponsoring bodies of PRAXIS, and organizes a younger liturgists' seminar and occasional conferences and consultations.

Information concerning the annual subscription, applications for membership, and lists of publications is obtainable from the treasurer, The Revd T. R. Barker, 11 Abbey Street, Chester CH1 2JF, England.